LEADING THE
IMPROVING DEPARTMENT

LEADING THE IMPROVING DEPARTMENT

*A HANDBOOK OF STAFF
DEVELOPMENT ACTIVITIES*

ALMA HARRIS

WITH **ANNE ALLSOP**
AND **NICK SPARKS**

David Fulton Publishers
London

David Fulton Publishers Ltd
Ormond House, 26–27 Boswell Street, London WC1N 3JZ
www.fultonpublishers.co.uk

First published in Great Britain in 2002 by David Fulton Publishers

Note: The right of Alma Harris to be identified as author of this work
has been asserted by her in accordance with the Copyright, Designs
and Patents Act 1988.

Copyright © 2002 Alma Harris

British Library Cataloguing in Publication Data
A catalogue record for this book is available from the British Library.

ISBN 1–85346–808–8 ✓

Typeset by Servis Filmsetting Ltd, Manchester
Printed in Great Britain by Bell and Bain Ltd, Glasgow

Contents

Contributors

Alma Harris is Professor of School Leadership at the Institute of Education, University of Warwick. She has published widely on the theme of subject leadership and her books include *Effective Subject Leadership*, David Fulton Publishers (1999).

Anne Allsop and **Nick Sparks** were both experienced deputy heads prior to becoming Local Education Authority (LEA) inspectors. Anne Allsop is currently Senior Inspector for Nottinghamshire LEA and Nick Sparks is Regional Director for the Teaching and Learning in the Foundation Subjects (TLF) stand of the National Key Stage 3 strategy.

Acknowledgements

This book reflects the work undertaken in the last few years with heads of department, subject leaders and LEA advisers throughout England and Wales. It encapsulates the evidence concerning departmental improvement and provides a range of related staff development activities. The book is based upon the growing research base concerning this important middle leadership role. It is also grounded in the practical experience of working with middle managers and running staff development programmes aimed at improving departments and subject areas.

The book has adopted the format of other highly successful books in the David Fulton staff development series.[1] In particular, the companion volume *Effective Subject Leadership* has influenced the structure and content of this book. It is hoped that this text plus *Effective Subject Leadership* will offer Heads of Department and subject leaders a coherent view of how to be more effective and how to improve their teams.

Department and subject level leadership is an important area for research and development. The National College for School Leadership is committed to developing a national programme for middle level leaders. The College also has an important research agenda that focuses upon improving leadership practice at all levels. I am fortunate to be working with Peter Newton, David Jackson and Collette Singleton and other colleagues at the National College in pursuing this important research and development agenda.

I am indebted to Anne Allsop and Nick Sparks for their intellectual and practical input to this book and very appreciative of the case study contributions from Jackie Parker and Paul Hammond. I am particularly grateful to Nina Stibbe of David Fulton Publishers for

---

[1] The following handbooks of staff development activities are available from David Fulton Publishers: *Creating the Conditions for Teaching and Learning; Improvements in the Quality of Education for All; Creating the Conditions for Classroom Improvement; Creating the Conditions for School Improvement;* and *Effective Subject Leadership in Secondary Schools.*

believing that a complementary handbook to *Effective Subject Leadership* was worth pursuing.

Finally, this book would not have been possible without the co-operation of the many teachers, subject leaders and Heads of Department that I continue to work with across the country. Their insights have informed the content of this book and their work reinforces the importance of placing teaching and learning at the heart of school and departmental improvement.

Alma Harris
The University of Warwick
January 2002

Chapter 1

Introduction

The pressure upon schools to improve and to raise achievement is unlikely to decrease in the next few years. Government policy remains firmly focused upon securing increased student and school performance. Leadership is acknowledged to be of central importance in the pursuit of even higher standards. The establishment of a National College for School Leadership represents a major investment in the professional development and training of school leaders and endorses their pivotal role in school improvement. Despite the concentration of effort and resources upon the leadership of the headteacher, research findings also indicate the importance of leadership at other levels within the school organisation (Day *et al*. 2000). Successive studies have shown that within effective schools, leadership extends beyond the senior management team to encompass other levels.

Within the current context, effective leadership is acknowledged to be of central importance in the pursuit of even higher standards. For schools that are improving, effective leadership has been shown to be a central and important component. However, until relatively recently the prime focus has been on the leadership of the headteacher and the senior management team. There is now substantial evidence to demonstrate that, while this leadership is necessary, it is often not sufficient to generate the capacity for sustained school improvement. Leadership at other levels has been shown to contribute significantly to school development and improvement.

One important source of leadership is found at the subject leadership level. In both primary and secondary schools, subject leaders are uniquely placed to influence the quality of teaching and learning within their subject areas. As team leaders they have a powerful influence over classroom practices and are important gatekeepers of change and development within their subject areas. The Subject Leader Standards acknowledge the centrality of the subject leader in contributing to whole school policy and development.

While the headteacher and governors carry overall responsibility for school improvement, a subject leader has responsibility for the subject curriculum and for establishing high standards of teaching and learning in their subject as well as playing a major role in the development of school policy. (TTA 1998:3)

The overall purpose of the subject leader's role is to contribute to school improvement and increased standards of performance through the provision of high quality teaching within the subject area. In order to achieve this, the subject leader has to lead and manage the curriculum and to respond to the internal and external demands for accountability and quality. All these demands have to be met in the particular context of the individual school and the community it serves.

Within a school the skills, abilities and expertise of subject leaders will inevitably vary. Differences exist between departments in terms of performance and effectiveness. However, it is possible to develop and improve leadership at this level through the provision of structured support. It has been shown that an optimum source of support resides in other subject leaders or Heads of Department within the school. By drawing upon the expertise and knowledge of those in middle management positions in the same context, the possibility of improvement across departments is significantly enhanced.

A changing leadership role

Since 1998 there has been a radical shift in the role and responsibilities of curriculum subject and departmental leaders. The Subject Leader Standards represent a major redefinition of role, expectations and performance of leaders at departmental and subject level. The 'National Standards for Subject Leaders' encompass ten dimensions of teaching and leadership:

- knowledge and understanding;
- planning and setting expectations;
- teaching and managing student learning;
- assessment and evaluation;
- student achievement;
- relations with parents and the wider community;
- managing own performance and development;
- managing and developing staff and other adults;
- managing resources;
- strategic leadership.

The Standards highlight the importance of high quality teaching and improved standards of achievement (TTA 1998). They also acknowledge the importance of establishing high standards of teaching and learning in their subject as well as playing a major role in the development of school policy (TTA 1998:3).

Consequently the scope and role of subject leaders have expanded quite dramatically. Subject and departmental leaders are now responsible for formulating and implementing policies for the subject or area of work; for devising short-, medium- and long-term plans; for setting challenging targets; for promoting effective practice and for reviewing progress. These activities involve all the staff who contribute to the subject area and will relate directly to the school's vision, policies, priorities and targets. Most importantly, subject and departmental leaders are responsible for ensuring that the teaching within the subject area is effective; that teaching is regularly and systematically monitored and evaluated; that student targets are set and that resources are efficiently used.

This leadership role now includes a diverse and pressing set of demands. In addition, there are some inherent tensions within the 'new' role that will require consideration. The new responsibilities placed upon subject and departmental leaders are extensive and exhaustive. In the majority of schools these responsibilities will prove difficult to fulfil because, unlike other school leaders, heads of department have a significant teaching responsibility that competes for time and energy. If subject or department leaders are to be able to work most effectively on behalf of their team members and the school, then additional time would seem to be an important prerequisite.

The National Standards make it clear that the role is primarily concerned with leadership rather than management. While leadership and management are often seen as inseparable concepts, the functions associated with each are clearly different. Subject and departmental leaders have an operational responsibility to ensure subject area objectives and targets are met and tasks are completed. These maintenance responsibilities are necessary to run an efficient department or subject area and represent the day-to-day management requirements of the role. In addition, subject or department leaders are also required to provide a vision for the subject area, to provide clear direction, to motivate others and to inspire and gain the commitment of those within their team. Such leadership qualities are necessary to develop the subject area, to improve achievement and to raise standards.

While subject and departmental leaders are very much in the front line, this does not necessarily mean that they are automatically involved in school-level decision-making. Levels of involvement vary according to the management approach of senior staff and the way in which both groups interact. In order to contribute to whole school development, subject or department leaders need to be participants in policy development and strategic planning. This requires, first, structural change where a formal 'two-way' equal relationship is established between middle and senior management and, second, cultural change where subject or department leaders are integrally involved in decision-making and policy developments within the school.

At the core of the subject or department leader's role is improving the quality of teaching and learning. This inevitably involves monitoring performance and evaluating the quality of teaching within the subject area. It also necessitates judging teaching ability and, if necessary, challenging 'poor' teaching and unacceptable classroom practices. With performance management, subject or department leaders have a more prominent role to play in evaluating teaching and will be increasingly called upon as a source of evidence about teaching ability and competence. Yet, subject or department leaders also have a major role to play in supporting colleagues within their subject area. As a team leader, their role is to foster trust and mutual support within the team. Consequently, the challenge facing subject and departmental leaders is how to foster a climate of change and innovation that leads to improved learning outcomes for students. The aim of this book is to assist subject and departmental leaders in meeting this challenge by instigating, leading and securing improvement within their team.

Who is the book for?

This book is intended for the Head of Department or subject leader who is interested in departmental level change and development. It will be of particular relevance to those subject or departmental leaders participating in the **national programme** for subject/ specialist leaders 'leading from the middle' or taking part in other high quality development opportunities. Essentially, the book is intended for Heads of Department or subject leaders who want to improve student achievement and performance through enhanced team working. The book is also a resource for those aspiring Heads of Department who want to know more about departmental leadership and improvement. Whatever the motivation for reading this book, its intention is to assist subject and departmental leaders to improve the quality of teaching and learning in their subject areas.

What is the aim of the book?

The aim of this book is to provide subject leaders with some practical guidance on change and improvement. The book offers an overview of those strategies and approaches that can be most easily incorporated into departmental and classroom practice within a wide range of subject areas. It also provides a series of staff development activities to allow subject and departmental leaders to explore improvement strategies and approaches in greater depth with their colleagues. In summary, the book provides ideas and materials to help subject and departmental leaders to build the capacity for improvement in teaching and learning to take place.

What does the book do?

The book allows subject and departmental leaders to consider a wide range of different approaches to development and change. To be most effective, subject and departmental leaders need to be constantly seeking to improve their leadership repertoire. This book provides suggestions, ideas and information on improving and extending leadership practice. It also offers a set of strategies and approaches for improving departmental performance.

The book is based on the research evidence concerning departmental effectiveness and improvement (Harris *et al.* 1995; Harris 1999; Busher and Harris 2000). It also draws upon the practical experience of a university- and LEA-led course for subject or department leaders.[1] The inputs, activities and advice offered during this staff development programme have been put to the test. Those that have been shown to work most effectively have been incorporated into this book.

Where do the ideas come from?

The book should be used as a guide and an introduction to development improvement and change. It provides a variety of starting points for subject or department leaders interested in extending their leadership repertoire by incorporating new approaches. Some subject and departmental leaders will want to start with those approaches that have the most direct applicability to their context. Others will want to investigate approaches that require thought, imagination and tenacity to use within their department or subject area. A key task of those using the suggestions and materials will be to decide how best to use the strategies and approaches for their department or subject area.

This book is essentially about building leadership capacity and improving the quality of teaching and learning within the department or subject area. It is a practical handbook and not a theoretical text, although it is well grounded in research evidence and based on practical evidence of 'what works'. It has been written to assist subject and departmental leaders in building the capacity for improvement within their subject areas. We hope that it will encourage subject and departmental leaders to engage their team members in change and innovation that will result in improved learning outcomes for all students.

How should the book be used?

[1] Leading the Improving Department – a course for subject leaders led by the University of Nottingham with Nottingham LEA and Nottinghamshire LEA (2000–1).

Chapter 2

Effective departments

The work by UK researchers (Harris *et al.* 1996, 1998; Sammons *et al.* 1997) suggests that heads of department can make a difference to performance in their subject areas in much the same way as headteachers contribute to overall school performance. The department as a sphere of influence has been termed the 'realm of knowledge' because of the importance of the subject boundary (Siskin 1994). Furthermore, it has been suggested that at the departmental level there is the major possibility of influencing whole school development.

Introduction

Research has revealed that there are features or characteristics which effective departments or subject areas consistently display (Harris 1999). While the complexity and uniqueness of each school context are acknowledged, it is generally recognised that the departmental level can contribute significantly to raised performance and achievement (Harris 2001). Consequently, there is a growing consensus on the need to focus upon teaching and learning issues at the departmental and the classroom level in order to raise standards.

Effective departments place student learning at the very centre of their work. They are primarily concerned with providing a challenging but caring environment for students. Effective departments are characterised by the emphasis they place upon involving students and generating the internal conditions for high quality learning to take place. These departments create a 'climate' for change or improvement. Such a climate exists where the department is committed to improvement and is prepared to change rather than adapt current practices. Developing this climate has been found to be a necessary prerequisite of effective departmental working. While externally imposed change or a new Head of Department can instigate the momentum for improvement, without a 'climate for change' departments will tend to modify and refine existing practices.

Effective departments can be identified by their clear and shared sense of vision. This vision is often shaped by the Head of Department's leadership style and can influence how teaching and learning are organised within the department. One of the most striking findings from the various research studies into departmental effectiveness has been the collegiate vision adopted by effective departments. Effective departments have been found to be 'talking departments', i.e. departments that are marked by a constant professional interchange both at a formal and informal level. Within effective departments meetings tend to focus on developmental issues as well as routine management matters. In short, effective departments operate in a collegiate way in order to improve their teaching. They tend to achieve this goal by basing their practice on the highest professional standards, often modelled by the Head of Department.

Features of effective department

The research evidence shows that effective departments tend to be those with the ability to organise key elements of teaching and learning in an optimum way. Effective departments tend to be organised and generate detailed and collectively agreed schemes of work which:

- reflect the departmental vision of 'good' practice in teaching and learning;
- are very detailed and offer clear guidance on teaching approaches;
- are regarded as important documents by departmental members and are easily accessible to all within the department;
- are collectively produced and agreed.

In order to translate these schemes of work into effective teaching and learning stategies, the **management of resources** within effective departments has been shown to be very important. Effective departments tend to manage their resources to the advantage of the whole department and to the advantage of all students. For example, one research project (Harris *et al.* 1995) describes how a science department decided to buy enough sets of basic equipment so that all students in that department could undertake the majority of experiments. In this way the department did not disadvantage any student or groups of students. Effective departments enhance learning for all students and this is often achieved through the optimum allocation of departmental resources.

Within effective departments **monitoring and evaluation** have been shown to be an important dual process. The mechanisms for monitoring student progress have been found to be tightly in place in departments that are improving. Information about the progress of individual students tends to be systematically collected through a variety of means and is shared within and across departments. In addition, effective departments are those that keep detailed profiles of students to chart individual progress. These profiles often include detailed assessments of students' strengths and weaknesses in the subject area and are regularly shared with students. Effective departments also know their own strengths and weaknesses and collect systematic evidence of their progress towards set departmental goals. Effective departments are departments which **'self-evaluate'** and place a high premium on both the process and outcomes of self-evaluation.

At the heart of any effective department is the effective organisation of **teaching and learning.** It is clear from the research findings that effective departments have certain set protocols in relation to teaching and learning. For example, the opportunity to offer students regular feedback on their progress has been shown to be central to the work of effective departments. Similarly, effective departments tend to take a great deal of time and effort to select what to teach their students. Effective departments find content and ways of teaching it which match the capacities and interests of their students.

Teaching and learning within effective departments are at an optimum when:

- students are fully involved in the learning process by being provided with a variety of tasks which deal with individual, small group, and large group situations;
- teachers encourage cooperative learning where students work together as part of a team sharing experiences, being given different roles and developing their own self-esteem;
- students are actively involved in a review of and reflection on the learning process;
- teachers develop meaningful, formative and motivational forms of assessment which reinforce and build confidence.

(Harris 1999)

Also, effective departments take care to translate the selected syllabus into carefully crafted schemes of work. Overall, effective departments are characterised by the care and attention they pay to the process of assessment. The assessment systems of effective departments have been found to include the following features:

- Detailed and up-to-date record keeping, e.g a sophisticated spreadsheet of student marks.
- Great stress placed upon trying to make marking consistent within the department.
- Efforts are made to try and give the students a stake in the assessment, e.g. they are often invited to mark each other's and their own work and to discuss their marks with the teacher in order to try and understand the strengths and weaknesses of their own efforts.
- The assessment system is used as the vehicle for frequent feedback to the students.
- Feedback tends to be more criterion than norm-referenced.

From the research findings concerning effective departments, a number of key features emerge. First, effective departments enjoy a **collegiate** management style and share a strong vision of their subject. Second, effective departments are well organised in terms of **assessment**, record keeping, homework, etc. and employ good resource management. Third, effective departments have efficient systems for **monitoring and evaluating** student progress that leads to structured and regular student feedback. Fourth, effective departments operate very **clear routines and practices** within lessons. There is an emphasis upon consistency and high quality practice. Finally, effective departments have a strong student-centred ethos that systematically rewards students and provides every opportunity for autonomous student learning. In short, effective departments are centrally concerned with **effective teaching and learning.**

Summary

Of all the variables under the control of the department, the quality of teaching has been shown to have the most demonstrable impact upon departmental performance. Departments that engage in professional dialogue on and development of teaching and learning are likely to be most effective. Similarly, where the Head of Department is the leading professional within the department, the possibility of departmental effectiveness and improvement is significantly increased.

Activity 2.1: enhancing departmental effectiveness

Effective departments display a consistent set of characteristics. Planning is an important dimension of departmental change and development.

Context

Aims

Briefing

- To consider the features of effective departments.
- To plan for departmental improvement and development.

Process

Step 1 involves using the features of effective departments to identify areas for departmental action and development. Step 2 expands upon those areas by considering the implications for change. Step 3 evaluates the extent to which the changes proposed will lead to departmental improvement.

Step 1   As a department consider the features of effective departments (opposite) and identify those features your department currently displays.

Which features does your department have?

Which features does your department need?

Which features require further development?

Identify areas for action and development

Features of effective departments (Harris *et al.* 1995)

- a collegiate management style;
- a strong vision of the subject effectively translated down to the level of the classroom;
- good organisation in terms of assessment, record keeping, homework, etc.;
- good resource management;
- an effective system for monitoring and evaluation;
- clear routines and practices within lessons;
- a strong pupil-centred ethos that systematically rewards pupils;
- opportunities for autonomous pupil learning;
- a central focus on teaching and learning.

Features associated with greater departmental effectiveness at GCSE (Sammons *et al.* 1997)

- High expectations
- Strong academic emphasis
- Shared vision/goals
- Clear leadership
- An effective SMT
- Consistency of approach
- Quality of teaching
- Focus on students
- Parental support/involvement

Step 2   Agree key areas for departmental action and development.

In order to address these key areas, what are the implications and next steps for the department?

Are there issues for whole school management?

Who needs to be informed?

Use the following checklist to gauge how far the plans made for departmental improvement are robust, realistic and will lead to improvements in teaching and learning.

Step 3

Enhancing departmental effectiveness

- Are actions firmly evidence based?
  (Are you sure you're doing what needs to be done?)

- Are teaching and learning at the heart of change?
  (Are you focusing on the most important thing – how effectively students learn?)

- Does the team know who does what?
  (Does everyone have clarity about roles?)

- Do actions involve the range of activity from 'awareness raising' to 'policy creation' to 'implementation'?
  (Does your plan move initiatives through to embedded practice?)

- Are training implications addressed?
  (Are you precise about who needs to be 'skilled up' and to what level?)

- Are whole school policies and developments reflected in the development?
  (Are you doing your 'bit' to contribute to whole school improvement?)

- Can success be readily judged?
  (Can you tell easily whether you have done what you said you would do?)

- Will impact upon students' 'entitlement' and 'achievements' be precisely identified?
  (Can you tell whether you have made a difference to the students?)

Chapter 3

Improving leadership

The quality of teaching and learning within a department or subject area is greatly influenced by the form of leadership adopted. Research has shown that effective departments or subject areas are both collegiate and cooperative and that this way of working is the result of a particular leadership style adopted by the subject leader or Head of Department (Harris 1999). The most typical leadership approach within an effective department or a subject area is that of the 'leading professional'. This is where the Head of Department is considered by other departmental members to be the model to follow. In short, he or she is viewed as an expert practitioner and is viewed by members of the department as a source of good practice. Effective leaders have a clear vision for the development of the subject area or department and have the ability to share this vision with colleagues to ensure that developments are taken forward.

Departments or subject areas that do not possess a clear or shared sense of vision about their work will be less effective. The leadership approach in less effective departments or subject areas falls into two extreme types. At one extreme, leadership is equated with having an **authoritarian style** controlling all aspects of departmental work. This leadership approach excludes team members from decision-making and leads to feelings of resentment because there is a lack of collaboration within the subject area or department. At the opposite extreme, leadership is characterised as *laissez-faire* where departmental responsibilities are delegated to others. This form of leadership places too much responsibility on others to complete and achieve tasks. It presents a lack of direction and responsibility for the work within the subject area or department. This form of leadership will prove to be detrimental because too much is asked of team members against a backdrop of inadequate leadership and a lack of direction. Neither of these two leadership styles will be conducive to effective working within subject areas or departments. Where leadership is authoritarian or 'too tight', team members will feel excluded and demoralised. Where leadership is *laissez-faire*, or 'too loose', team

Introduction

members will be overburdened, rudderless and resentful (Harris 1998).

The dimensions of the leadership role

Drawing upon the work of Busher and Harris (1999), it is possible to identify four dimensions of the leadership role. The first concerns a **bridging** or **brokering** function. This implies a **transactional leadership** role for the subject or departmental leader. In this role, Heads of Department make use of power – usually 'power over' others – to attempt to secure working agreements with departmental colleagues about how to achieve school and departmental goals and practices. Part of this role is the managing and allocating of resources available to the department.

A second dimension focuses on how subject and departmental leaders encourage staff to cohere and develop a group identity. The area of subject knowledge that the department shares usually defines the boundaries of the group. An important role for the leader, therefore, is to foster **collegiality** within the group by shaping and establishing a shared vision. This necessarily implies a leadership style that empowers others. This style of leadership is people-oriented and requires a leadership approach that helps other people to transform their feelings, attitudes and beliefs. Transformational leaders not only manage structure but also purposefully impact upon the culture in order to change it.

A third dimension of effective leadership concerns the **improvement of staff and student performances**. At one level this implies a transactional leadership role for the Head of Department in monitoring the attainment of school goals and meeting particular prescribed levels of curriculum performance. On the other hand, it suggests an important mentoring or supervisory leadership role in supporting colleagues' development and the development of students academically and socially.

The fourth and final dimension of effective leadership is a **liaison** or **representative role**. This requires the subject or department leader to be in touch with a variety of actors and sources of information in the external environment of the school and to negotiate, where necessary, on behalf of the other members of the department. Part of this dimension is representing the views of colleagues to the senior staff and to others within the school.

These four dimensions of the subject or departmental leadership role are both complementary and potentially competing in their demands. They reflect the complexity of the leadership role and, most importantly, that leadership is essentially about **relationships**. Subject and departmental leaders need to understand that there are three main types of elements interacting within the leadership process: the leader, the followers and the situation.

Leaders create situations or exploit situations within which team members can be innovative and creative. Leaders also encourage growth and development in their followers. They are interested in the professional development of others and in maximising the potential of those within their team. Leadership is essentially the process of building and maintaining a sense of vision, culture and interpersonal relationships, whereas management is the coordination, support and monitoring of organisational activities.

The practice of effective leadership is underpinned by a number of core **personal values**. These concern the promotion of respect (for individuals), fairness and equality, caring for the well-being and whole development of students and staff, integrity and honesty. This sense of caring and belief in staff is the key to successful improvement efforts and is at the core of effective leadership. The two principal concerns of effective leaders are maintaining teacher morale and building capacity for improvement. An emphasis on the continuing development of staff is important as it is a clear recognition that teachers are the most important asset within the department or subject area.

The most important aspect of leadership is working successfully with **people**. By definition, good leaders are not only enthusiastic about their jobs and the potential and achievements of the organisation in which they work, they are also believers in their own judgement. They are ruthless in their establishment of high expectations, aware of the need to think strategically so that they can position their department or subject area to be one step ahead of emerging changes. This means a continuing pressure on self and others for improvement based upon existing intrinsic values. It is in the combination of values, attitudes, skills and qualities where the means of achieving the best for staff and students is revealed, rather than in any single leadership strategy or personal trait.

In summary, effective subject and departmental leaders:

- focus upon the care and achievement of students simultaneously;
- create, maintain and constantly monitor relationships within the department or subject area;
- seek, synthesise and evaluate internal and external data to improve performance;
- persist with apparently intractable issues in their drive for higher standards;
- are prepared to take risks in order to achieve these;
- are not afraid to ask difficult questions of themselves and others;
- are not afraid to acknowledge failure but are willing to learn from it;
- are aware of a range of sources to help solve problems;
- manage ongoing tensions and dilemmas in a principled way;
- are clear in their vision for the department/subject area and communicate this to all staff and students.

In the literature on effective leadership, increasing emphasis is placed upon the importance of leaders having a **vision** for the department or subject area. This implies that subject or departmental leaders have a clear image of where they would like their team to be. In order to 'build' a vision, subject and departmental leaders need to have a clear view of the current performance and culture of the team. This will involve asking such questions as:

- How is the department/subject area currently performing?
- Where are its main strengths and weaknesses?
- Where would I like the department/subject area to be?
- Where would my colleagues like the department/subject area to be?
- How do we create a vision together?
- How do we work towards this vision?

Visions have to be shared and lived by those within the team, including the leader who will have a major role in reinforcing the vision to others. One way of articulating the vision for the department or subject area is to create a 'vision statement' that reflects the values and beliefs that team members hold. The essential feature of a vision statement is that it conveys a clear image of what the department or subject area wishes to work towards. An example of a vision statement is provided below:

> The English department is committed to ensuring that students enjoy, appreciate and value learning all aspects of the subject and achieve the best they can in every lesson.

A vision is a picture of a future reality and implies that there is something to progress towards and goals to be met. Research has shown that highly effective departments have a clear vision and a shared set of values (Harris *et al*. 1995). Conversely, ineffective departments are characterised by a lack of vision and a lack of shared values (Harris 1998). Consequently, effective leadership involves:

- establishing a clear vision for the department/subject area;
- being seen to demonstrate these values in practice;
- having clear goals and targets for departmental improvement;
- working with others to achieve these goals and targets;
- translating the core vision and values into day-to-day practicalities.

Vision building within a department or subject area has been shown to promote learning within the team. However, it is important that the vision is meaningful to others, achievable and realistic. In this way progress can be charted and recognised. Unrealistic goals and expectations may cause frustration and resentment within the team and be counter-productive to development and improvement.

Improving leadership

There are a number of ways in which leadership can be developed and improved. It is important that subject and departmental leaders take time to reflect upon their experiences and to consider what aspect of their leadership behaviour requires attention or modification. The following are ways in which leadership can be enhanced or improved:

- *Obtaining feedback.* In order to improve leadership skills and qualities it is important for leaders to obtain relevant feedback. If leaders are not given any feedback from their leadership experiences, then valuable learning will be lost. For departmental and subject leaders it is important that those working with them provide feedback. This can be achieved in meetings, or in a one-to-one discussion or through an evaluative tool such as a questionnaire. It is important that the feedback is provided and received in a spirit of mutual respect and honesty.

  Constructive feedback is:

  - helpful
  - specific
  - based on evidence
  - timely
  - accurate
  - individual
  - direct
  - developmental
  - without blame.

  The role of an effective subject leader is to create a culture or 'climate' that enables and ensures that feedback is positive and focused on professional development and improvement.

- *Learning from others.* Leaders learn from others by asking questions and paying attention to how others respond to everyday situations. Leaders can learn a lot by observing how others react to and handle different challenges and situations. It is also possible to learn from others by asking them to articulate why they took a certain action or responded in a certain way. To learn from others it is important to understand the motivation and beliefs that influence certain actions and behaviour.

- *Personal development planning.* Leadership development almost certainly occurs in ways that are not always anticipated or controlled. A systematic plan outlining personal goals and strategies will help departmental and subject leaders take advantage of opportunities or experiences that they might otherwise overlook. Having a personal development plan will help leaders to prioritise and to seek out opportunities that will be of most benefit to them. A first step in planning ahead is being clear about what your personal goals and aspirations are and prioritising these against competing demands. Leaders who are clear about their own personal goals are more likely to have a clear vision of where they and their colleagues are heading.

- *Managing stress.* The term stress is used in a number of different ways. Sometimes it is used to mean particular sorts of environmental conditions such as being in a stressful job in difficult conditions. It can also be used to describe the symptoms a person is experiencing such as muscular tension, headache or difficulty concentrating. Stress often occurs in situations that are overly complex, demanding, unclear, dangerous or threatening. The stressfulness of any event depends on how it is interpreted or responded to, rather than on the event itself. Managing stress involves keeping things in perspective and trying to avoid blame, panic or loss of control. It necessitates recognising that stress is a response to a situation and is not inherent in the situation itself. It is also important for subject and departmental leaders to acknowledge the stress of others, particularly those with whom they work most closely. Effective leaders are those who make sure that they recognise the stress others are under without becoming an additional source of stress.

- *Building effective relationships*. In order to be an effective leader it is important that you build effective relationships with those you lead. It is possible for subject or departmental leaders to have authority without influence in the respect that they have **authority** as leaders but do not have personal **influence** to bring about change. By building positive relationships it is more likely that the subject or departmental leaders can exert an influence over others. This can be achieved through recognising common interests, goals and understanding. It can also be secured through understanding colleagues' tasks, problems and rewards. Effective leaders create, cultivate and sustain positive relationships with others even though differences of opinion, personality and viewpoint might exist. If the leader focuses on the positive aspects of the team and has respect for team members, it will be more possible to build effective relationships.

Summary

Within improving departments and subject areas the quality of leadership and the leadership style are critically important. Effective leaders have a vision and demonstrate a consistent set of values to those in their team. They enable their teams to translate that vision and set of values into practical day-to-day actions or activities. They also spend time investing in their own leadership skills and in building positive relationships with others.

Activity 3.1: creating effective leaders

It is clear from the research evidence that leadership is an important contributor to departmental improvement. But how do leaders become more effective?

Context

Aim

Briefing

To consider the characteristics of effective leadership.

Process

Step 1 involves the department or group considering the list of characteristics of effective team leadership and placing them in order of priority, first individually and then as a group. Step 2 requires individuals to evaluate the various approaches to leadership. Step 3 matches different leadership approaches to specific contexts. Step 4 considers the ways in which leadership competency is enhanced and developed.

Step 1   In pairs, place the following list of characteristics of effective team leadership in order of priority, first individually and then as a group. Add any other characteristics that you feel are missing or are not fully represented in the list.

Characteristics of effective team leadership

- Commitment to the task

- A clearly stated brief

- Agreed levels of delegated authority

- Adequate resources and service support

- Agreed ground rules

- A feasible time-scale

- Readjustment of existing workloads during the period of the project

- Agreed success criteria

-

-

-

-

Individually, now consider the following three approaches to leadership. Have you experienced all three forms of leadership? Which proved most effective?

Authoritarian, democratic and *laissez-faire* leadership

Authoritarian	Democratic	*Laissez-faire*
Tells people what to do	Directs or supports people as necessary	Does not like directing people
Keeps information from team members	Shares information of relevance to the team	Shares information unnecessarily
Stifles debate	Plans well-structured meetings which allow for debate but reach decisions	Allows so much debate that clear decisions are rarely made
Tightly controls meetings		Allows meetings to drag on
Gives the impression that decisions are made before they are discussed	Agrees clear procedures with the team	Lacks procedures
Employs rigid procedures	Has a clear philosophy but listens to other views	Gives the impression of having no clear philosophy for the team
Seems to have 'tunnel vision'		
Fails to develop colleagues by refusing to delegate	Develops colleagues by negotiating the delegation of some tasks	Fails to develop colleagues by not planning delegation

---

Step 3   Different situations call for different leadership styles. In pairs, decide what types of situation would require the following leadership styles.

Situational leadership styles

Directing	Coaching	Supporting	Delegating
The leader provides very clear and specific direction and closely monitors results achieved	The leader directs and supervises, but also explains decisions, encourages suggestions and supports progress	The leader facilitates and supports team members in decision-making and accomplishing tasks	The leader delegates responsibility for decision-making and task completion to team members

---

Step 4   As a department or group, discuss how different leadership approaches could be developed and shared within the subject team.

Chapter 4

Improving the team

The subject or departmental team is an important sphere of influence within the school. For most teachers this is the team they relate to on a daily basis and to which they have most loyalty. However, when a team fails to function in a positive way there can be serious repercussions for the performance of that team. Studies of ineffective schools and departments have shown how dysfunctional relationships within teams can negatively affect the quality of teaching and learning. Teams that fail to work together spend a large amount of energy working against each other. Therefore, it is the responsibility of the team leader to invest in team building even if the team is working relatively well.

Not only do teams vary in the specialised roles or tasks they undertake but they also vary in their effectiveness. Successful and less successful teams can be differentiated in terms of certain key characteristics. First, effective teams have a clear mission and shared set of goals. Everyone in the team knows what the team is trying to achieve and shares a vision of how to achieve their shared goals. Effective team leadership involves assessing resources within the team and evaluating individual performance. Good team leaders also secure additional resources in order that the team may work most effectively.

Effective teams do the following:

- share a view of the goals they seek to achieve;
- convert the goals into a set of agreed tasks;
- identify what will count as success criteria in meeting the goals;
- actively listen to the suggestions and ideas of others;
- are aware of the parameters of the authority granted to the team;
- agree a set of procedures appropriate to the achievement of the task(s);
- assign appropriate functional roles in relation to the task;
- review progress and promote learning within the group;
- are able to deal with disagreements in a constructive way . . .

Introduction

- meet their goals in the allotted time-scales;
- evaluate their strengths and weaknesses in the light of results achieved.

High performance teams

Teams that perform well spend time planning and organising in order to make optimal use of resources. They also communicate effectively and have good inter-personal relationships. By working together in a positive way the potential for conflict is reduced and interpersonal differences are minimised. There are a number of key variables that need to be in place if a team is going to work efficiently and effectively:

- *Task structure* – does the team know what its task is?
- *Group boundaries* – is the group membership appropriate for the task?
- *Norms* – does the team share an appropriate set of norms for working as a team?
- *Authority* – has the team leader established a climate in which members of the team feel empowered to provide expert assistance when needed?
- *Shared goals* – do team members follow the same goals?

Having shared goals is the most important way in which teams are identified. This is why it is important that the departmental or subject leader has a clear vision and sense of purpose. However, leading and managing a subject team is complex. Teamwork is not about conformity and compliance. Instead, effective team working involves cooperation, sharing and mutual respect. The departmental or subject leader, therefore, is instrumental in building a team spirit and ethos that are supportive and conducive to change. This will not happen by accident but will be the result of team building and the departmental or subject leader recognising the different strengths of each member of the team.

Improving the team

Subject or department leaders need to reflect carefully on how they can use the strengths of the teachers and other staff in their teams. Hence the initial task of any subject or department leader must be to ensure that the department works and functions as an effective team. This may involve reconstituting and redefining the collective identity of a group of people so that they begin to perform as a team. According to Handy (1976), this involves the subject or department leader in taking the group through four specific phases of team development:

- *Forming* – The purpose of the team, its composition and organisation are discussed. Individuals establish their identities within the team and their positions within the group.
- *Storming* – Handling conflicts and challenges by individual members as clearer functions and roles are identified.

- *Norming* – Establishing norms and practices, including decisions on how work will be carried out.
- *Performing* – The group starts to work coherently and interdependently to achieve its goals.

The position of the subject or department leader means that they have a complicated set of interpersonal relationships to deal with in their teams. It is important, therefore, that subject or department leaders set clear parameters within which to work with others. For example, they need to ensure that all intrusions on their time have an agreed time limit, purpose and agenda. To develop **commitment** in others, subject or department leaders need to:

- involve staff in developing a clear sense of purpose;
- allow them to identify their own targets;
- encourage staff to take ownership of their work;
- value staff and maximise their potential within the subject area;
- praise and reward staff;
- celebrate success;
- devolve leadership responsibilities within the team.

One of the ways in which teams or communities work together is through formal **meetings**. Formal meetings have their own particular dynamics. One of the questions that a subject or department leader has to decide is which people need to attend what meeting. If staff are expected to attend meetings about students or procedures with which they are not involved, they are likely to perceive the meeting as a waste of time, harming the quality of discussion in the meeting and the quality of relationships between staff. Most importantly, subject or department leaders will need to be aware of their own and their colleagues' personal and professional views and interests in the matters under discussion. This understanding of people can help them chair a meeting or coordinate a discussion effectively. Subject or department leaders should ensure that:

- Meetings start on time, and their duration is clear.
- The purpose and content of the meeting are made clear.
- The feelings and understandings of staff members are regularly checked.
- Latecomers should be brought up to date.
- Members' contributions are respected and valued.
- Members are listened to, encouraged, supported.
- Differences and conflicts are talked out thoroughly.
- Questions and concerns are clarified.
- Participation is acknowledged and not taken for granted.

(Day *et al.* 1998)

Effective Heads of Department also enhance team meetings by clearly signalling how each item or issue is to be handled; reviewing the outcomes of discussions; agreeing or confirming the follow-up which is to take place and routinely evaluating the effectiveness of the process and outcomes of team meetings.

Another important component of team improvement is understanding and influencing the **motivation** of those within the team. The most effective way to determine what team members find intrinsically motivating is simply to ask them what they like to do. However, many team leaders either do not have particularly good relationships with team members or assume they know what motivates them, so they often fail to ask this straightforward but significant question. While it might not be possible to completely align tasks with the intrinsic interests of members of the team, it may be possible to allocate tasks so that they reflect the strengths and interests of team members.

Subject or departmental leaders should consider:

- What factors motivate or de-motivate others within my team?
- How far are these factors within my control?
- How do I allocate tasks within the team?
- Do I take individual motivation into account?
- How do I motivate others?
- Is there anything I could be doing to motivate team members?

Finally, it is important for teams to have a shared set of standards or an agreed framework to work within. This needs to be generated and agreed by all team members. This set of standards or quality framework will include the clear demarcation of roles and responsibilities within the team.

Team roles

Team roles are sets of expected behaviours associated with a particular task or responsibilities. Most teachers have multiple roles stemming from the various demands placed upon them from within the school and within their subject or departmental area. Effective leaders have two broad functions. One deals with getting the **task** done, the other concerns supporting **relationships** within the work group. Similarly, group roles can be characterised in terms of **task and role** functions.

Task roles in groups
Initiating
Informing
Information sharing
Summarising
Evaluating
Guiding

Relationship roles
Harmonising
Encouraging
Monitoring
Trouble-shooting
Motivating

Managing all these different roles is the responsibility of both the group leader and team members. These roles contribute to the overall effectiveness of the group and are important if the group is to work as a cohesive team. Where these roles are not undertaken, group performance is impeded. Within ineffective teams dysfunctional relationships are frequently observed. The research by Harris (1998) found that ineffective departments were those where personal relationships were dysfunctional and where communication had broken down severely.

One feature of ineffective team working is role conflict. Role conflict involves receiving contradictory messages about expected behaviour and can negatively affect personal well-being and performance. It is important that the subject or departmental leader is aware of potential role conflict and acts quickly to offset negative behaviour. Role conflict can occur in several ways. Perhaps most commonly it can occur when people receive inconsistent signals about expected behaviour from the same person. So, if the departmental or subject leader sends team members mixed messages about their performance and behaviour, this could promote role conflict and damage working relationships.

A major source of conflict can occur when there are inconsistencies in the different roles people undertake. For example, inter-role conflict occurs when someone is unable to perform all the roles to their satisfaction. For subject or departmental leaders this particular source of conflict is very familiar, particularly in view of the many roles required of them, i.e. teacher, manager, leader, administrator. Other sources of role conflict occur when there is role ambiguity, where messages about the role are not consistent or congruent. Also, there is personal role conflict when the behaviours required for the job are inconsistent with personal beliefs and values.

Within a team, different **dysfunctional behaviours** may be prevalent:

- dominating – monopolising time, enforcing personal views;
- blocking – obstructing, impeding group work, persistent negativity;
- attacking – aggressive, dismissive of others' views;
- passive – resisting by non-involvement;
- distracting – engaging in irrelevant behaviours, distracting others.

The subject or departmental leader may need to deal with some or all of these behaviours within their team. It is important for leaders to be able to minimise the degree to which these dysfunctional roles, role conflict and role ambiguity occur in their groups. Many subject or departmental leaders inherit teams that are dysfunctional and one of the main tasks, therefore, is to work with the team to offset negative behaviour. In order to create group cohesion, subject or departmental leaders will need to consider the following sets of questions:

- What negative behaviours are demonstrated in the team?
- How do I offset these behaviours?
- What positive behaviour should I be modelling?
- How do I change the norms within the group?
- How do I create alternative forms of behaviour?
- How do I create opportunities for team members to work together?
- How do I ensure that all team members feel valued?

If the subject or departmental leader finds that the team has a clear sense of vision and direction and that relationships within the team are based on mutual respect, even if personality differences exist, the team is more likely to be effective.

Summary

It is important that subject and departmental leaders understand how a team's sense of identity, common goals, level of task interdependence and differentiated roles affect functional and dysfunctional team behaviour. For departments or subject areas to be most effective, they need to work together, to share a common vision and common goals. The subject or departmental leader needs to ensure that teams generate and work towards a common set of quality standards.

Effective teams share common goals and work towards a shared set of standards. It is important that teams know how to generate their own 'quality standards'.

Context

Aim

Briefing

To generate and establish an agreed set of 'quality standards' within the department or subject area.

Process

This activity takes place in two steps. Step 1 requires teams or departments to familiarise themselves with the worked example. Step 2 requires teams or departments to use the worked example as a template to develop their own quality standards.

As a team or department work through the example provided. Note that the example incorporates the following headings: beliefs, aims, observable practice and targets.

Step 1

As a team or in smaller groups, focus on a number of common beliefs shared within the team. These might focus upon:

Step 2

- student learning
- effective teaching of the subject
- student motivation
- assessment
- monitoring and evaluation

Use the template in Figure 4.1 to generate aims, observable practice and targets. These will provide the basis for further discussion and for the agreement of 'quality standards' within the department or subject area.

Worked example

BELIEF   AIM   →   VERIFIABLE   →   TARGETS   →
                                 OBSERVABLE/
                                 TRANSLATION
                                 INTO PRACTICE

                                                                    50% of all lessons include
                                                                    differentiation by task
                                                                    for the more able

                                 More able students
                                 regularly undertake
                                 more challenging
                                 difficult work in   80% of all lessons include
                                 lessons and homework   high order skills (e.g. problem
                                                                    solving, hypothesis testing)

To stretch the
more able
students in our
classes   All questioning includes
                                                                    'speculative' and 'what if …'
                                                                    questions

Each child should
be set work
appropriate to
their abilities

Figure 4.1 Developing agreed quality standards

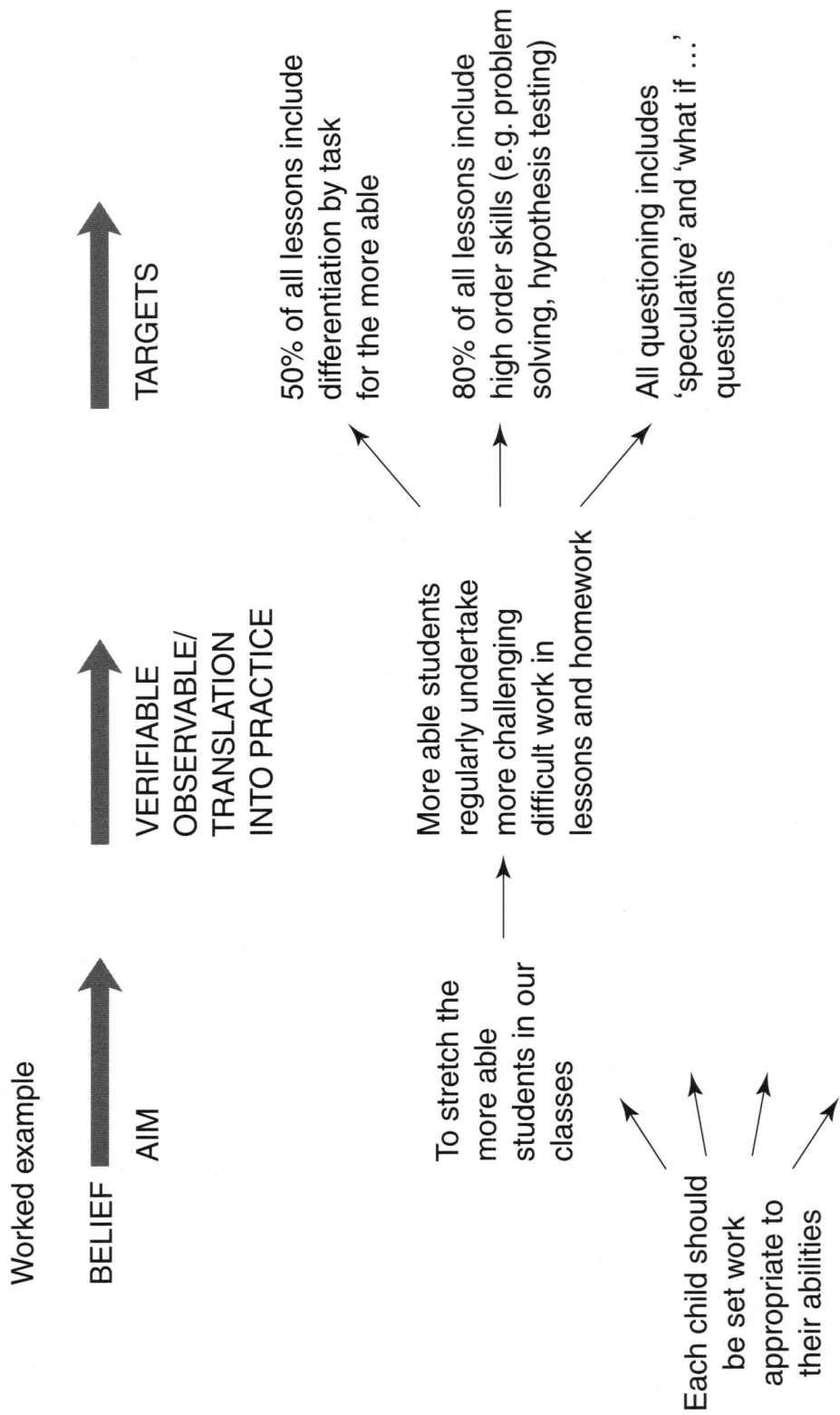

Belief

Aims

Therefore our aims are

Verifiable/observable practice
These will be achieved/demonstrated by translation into day-to-day practice, e.g.

Chapter 5

Improvement and change

One core responsibility of the subject or department leader is to create a climate for change and to manage the change process. This inevitably involves the management of innovation as leadership is essentially about inspiring others and enhancing their talents, energies and commitment. This necessitates developing and sustaining a shared vision, communicating shared values and motivating those within the team to accept and implement change.

A major reason for the failure of change at both school and subject area level lies in a lack of careful attention to the process of change. There are numerous barriers to the successful implementation of change that largely are found in the experience of change by those encountering it. In responding to change a great deal depends upon the way in which the change is presented. If departmental or subject leaders want to encourage others to participate in change to aid development, the change has to be presented in a positive way.

Introduction

In presenting change to colleagues, departmental or subject leaders need to consider how others will view the change. Will they see it as a threat, as unnecessary, as yet more work? Such responses to change are not unusual, yet they can undermine the process of change, however well intentioned. The first rule of securing successful change is to ensure others are **clear** about the intentions or purposes of the change. The second rule is to **involve** others in early discussions about the planned change, so they feel part of any proposed change, even though they may not approve of it. The third rule of change is to be prepared to accept **feedback**. If you are involving others in discussions about change, then they will have views, opinions and suggestions to offer. It is important, therefore, that all feedback, however critical, is accepted in a positive way. This does not mean detracting from the change but simply acknowledging the viewpoints of others and accepting helpful suggestions.

The fourth rule of change is not to take **resistance** personally. Resistance is a natural part of the change process. It does not equate

The rules of successful change

with defiance or recalcitrance but is simply a natural response to being asked to do something new or to do something differently. When faced with changes such as moving job, getting married or moving house, for example, most people experience some feelings of resistance. It is understandable why teachers might prefer to remain where they are secure, confident and sure of the terrain, rather than move into an unknown area which might potentially challenge or test their competence or performance. Consequently, it is important that departmental or subject leaders do not misread the signals from staff who are simply responding in a predictable way to the change process.

The fifth rule of change involves departmental or subject leaders anticipating **threats** to change. In order to secure successful change, the opportunities and threats need to be considered. One way of achieving this is for departmental and subject leaders to rehearse the threats the proposed changes might bring. This can be done using a simple SWOT analysis. For example, a Head of Department wishes to introduce peer observation into the department. Here is the SWOT analysis of this change.

Strengths	Weaknesses
Sharing good practice across the department	No experience of this within school
Improved teaching and learning	Split site
	Cover
Opportunities	**Threats**
Performance management – need for evidential base	Ofsted approaching
New member of staff – induction	Opportunity cost
	No support from SMT

Having completed such an analysis it is then possible to anticipate the threats and to present the positive aspects of the change to staff. Having thought through the dimensions of change, departmental and subject leaders will then be more able to argue for the change they require.

The sixth rule is to **plan** the process of change systematically and deliberately. While all departmental improvement requires change, not all change equates with improvement, therefore care needs to be taken with the types of changes that are introduced. Unplanned, ill-thought-through change will lead to negative comments. Consequently, it is important to follow the six rules of change and to ensure that change is not *ad hoc* or simply unrealistic.

The six rules of successful change are:

- Be clear about intentions.
- Involve others.
- Be prepared to accept feedback.
- Do not take resistance personally.

- Anticipate threats.
- Plan ahead.

In order to bring about successful change departmental and subject leaders will need to think about a number of issues or questions before engaging others in the change process.

- Is change necessary at this time?
- What is driving the change?
- What are the purposes of the intended change?
- Have all staff been consulted about the change?
- Is there evidence rather than opinion about the need for change?
- Will I have the support of the SMT?
- Are additional resources needed?
- Is specialist training required?
- What are the intended outcomes of this change?
- How will the change be evaluated?
- What will constitute success?

For change to be successful, departmental and subject leaders need to understand the process of change. Change can be complex, messy and unpredictable in its consequences, therefore it is important to understand that change is a process rather than an event or stand alone activity. If change is well managed, it will ensure that within the department or subject area it is seen as a necessary part of improvement.

The process of change

The change process is often thought of as linear and rational but in reality it is iterative and messy. As most change involves the interaction of others, it can become rather unpredictable and in some cases, uncontrollable. In Fullan's (1991) view, the change process has three major components:

- initiation
- implementation
- institutionalisation

These three components are not mutually exclusive but suggest that there are different stages within the whole change process. In order for subject or department leaders to manage the change process effectively it is important not only to understand what each phase involves but also to consider how they interrelate. The first of the three phases of change is the initiation stage.

Initiating change

As the word implies, the initiation phase is the point at which the proposed change is introduced to the department or subject area. There may be various routes to this initiation stage. For example, the proposed change may emerge from a departmental review, be imposed by the senior management team or may result from a problem within the department. The particular source of the change is important because it will have a direct effect on the way in which the change is introduced, understood and implemented.

As noted earlier, where teachers are kept informed of proposed changes and are part of the decision-making process, a greater sense of commitment and support for the change is generated. It may not always be possible for subject or department leaders to keep all team members informed of every discussion or development but where important and major changes are concerned, the primacy of access to information cannot be overstated.

It is clear that departmental development and improvement occur when teachers:

- engage in frequent, continuous and concrete talk about teaching practice;
- frequently observe and provide feedback to each other;
- plan, design and evaluate teaching materials together;
- work together in the change process.

Where such norms of collaborative practice are not in place, innovation and the initiation of change become more difficult to achieve. Consequently, where possible, subject or department leaders should encourage and plan for teachers to work together. This may not be always easy to achieve because of the constraints of time, resources and competing priorities. However, if teachers are able to work together, a more collaborative culture is generated and in this way the implementation of change is more likely to succeed.

Implementing change

The implementation stage is where planning stops and where action commences. Whether or not a change happens in practice is largely dependent upon the quality of implementation where the change or innovation is put into practice. For subject or department leaders, the main tasks during the implementation phase are the carrying out of action plans, developing and sustaining commitment, checking progress and overcoming any problems. During this phase there will be a need for a combination of pressure on and support for teachers from the subject or department leader. There has to be enough pressure to ensure that the momentum of change continues and that action takes place. Also, there needs to be sufficient technical, emotional and professional support to ensure that team members feel equipped to take on the various tasks related to the change. All change will place some stress on individuals so it is particularly important that departmental and team leaders support staff as much as possible through the implementation stage (see Figure 5.1).

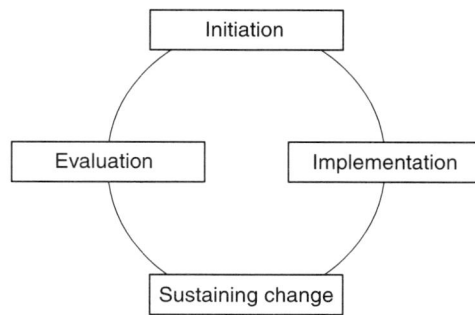

Figure 5.1   The process of change
Source: Fullan (1991)

During the implementation phase there will be a crucial time when the change appears to be making little progress. Fullan (1991) has termed this the 'implementation dip' which is inevitable in most change processes (see Figure 5.2).

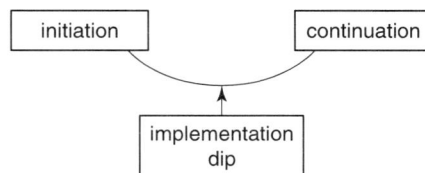

Figure 5.2   The implementation dip
Source: Fullan (1991)

Subject or department leaders need to recognise that this is an intrinsic part of the change process and does not mean that the change has failed. Instead, it indicates that the change is at a critical stage and that additional effort is required to mobilise the change. With each successive change, subject or department leaders and their team members will be more skilled in the change process and more able to ensure that the changes implemented are sustained and continued.

Sustaining change

This is the phase where the change is not regarded as being anything new because it has been embedded into the systems and culture of the subject area or department. While it might be assumed that this will happen automatically, in practice it requires that the change is monitored and evaluated to ensure that it is making the intended impact and that this impact is sustained. The role of the subject or department leader will be to ensure that appropriate monitoring and evaluation mechanisms are put in place to provide feedback not only on the initial impact of the change but also on the extent to which it is still in operation as intended.

Evaluating change

Whatever the impetus for change, it necessitates careful planning and systematic evaluation in order to succeed. Evaluation provides a basis upon which the subject or department leader is able to make judgements and informed decisions. While definitions of evaluation may vary, in essence, evaluation is the process of systematically collecting and analysing information in order to make informed judgements based upon sound evidence (English and Harris 1987). Using this definition, it is evident that the validity of the judgements made is highly dependent upon the nature and the provenance of the data collected.

Formative feedback is important because it provides the basis for altering aspects of the change/development as it is taking place. It also provides an early warning system that problems are being encountered and hindering successful implementation. This evaluation feedback allows the subject or department leader to problem-solve and to make decisions about fine-tuning or altering aspects of the change/development on the basis of evidence rather than on the basis of intuition.

Subject or department leaders might ask the following questions at the initiation stage:

- How well is the change/development being introduced?
- What is the evidence of success to date?
- What are the major barriers?
- How might these be overcome?
- Are any changes/modifications required?

A cycle of review, planning and action lies at the heart of improving schools and subject areas. Therefore, an evidence-based approach to managing change is vital to the development and the continued success of a subject area. The evaluative questions that can assist the subject or department leader in making judgements about the impact of the change might include:

- What has been the main impact of the change/development?
- Have there been any unintended outcomes?
- To what extent has the change led to improvements in teaching and learning within the subject area or department?
- What have we learned as a result of introducing this change?

Subject or departmental leaders therefore have a role to play in not only ensuring evaluation takes place but that their team members are part of the evaluation process.

The purpose of evaluation is to make judgements in order to inform practice. To do this it needs to be an integral part of what happens within subject areas, a positive and encouraging aspect of the work being undertaken. The key aims of any judgement about the impact of a change or of departmental performance should be to provide indications of what works well and what needs to be improved. Evaluation should also lead to further development. It should provide a basis for departmental and subject leaders to set strategic priorities and to highlight areas for future development.

The process of change will require departmental and subject leaders to actively support colleagues. The experience of change, as noted earlier, may be quite daunting so emotional, technical and professional support will be needed. Part of this support will involve professional development opportunities to assist staff to become skilled in the various areas needed to secure successful change. There are various methods of professional learning including the following:

- action research
- distance learning
- INSET
- job shadowing
- teacher placement
- personal reflection
- collaborative learning
- specialist courses
- lesson observation
- collaborative planning
- demonstration

It is important that any professional development opportunity meets departmental or subject needs as well as individual needs. The following are reasons why individuals may embark on professional development:

- to enhance their capability in their job;
- to work with others in a similar role;
- to obtain perspective on the work role;
- to obtain new experiences and new learning;
- to enable them to cope with and manage change most effectively.

It is important that departmental and subject leaders recognise that professional development can serve both individual and team needs. It is also important that professional development makes links between the workshop and workplace. The **workshop**, which is equivalent to the best practice on the traditional INSET course, is where understanding and knowledge are obtained. The **workplace** is the classroom and school where understanding and knowledge are applied.

The research evidence shows that teachers' ability to apply knowledge to a range of situations requires support from both within and outside the department. This implies creating opportunities for

Supporting colleagues

43

immediate and sustained practice alongside collaboration and peer coaching. It is important that the subject or departmental leader provides structured support to ensure that any professional development opportunity impacts upon the classroom and improves the quality of teaching and learning.

Summary

Subject and departmental improvement necessitates engaging in the process of change. In order to initiate and implement change most effectively, subject and departmental leaders need to offer their team members both challenge and support. The provision of evaluative feedback will ensure that subject and departmental leaders can gauge how well changes are being implemented and can assess the impact of the change on relevant aspects of departmental performance.

Activity 5.1: preparing for change

All departmental improvement involves change. When considering a focus for change it is important to consider areas of strength as well as weakness.

Aim

To identify areas of strength and weakness within the department/subject area as a means of setting priorities/goals for change.

Process

Step 1 involves using Figure 5.3 to identify strengths and weaknesses within the department or subject area. Step 2 involves identifying and prioritising areas for change and development. Step 3 focuses upon the priorities for change and involves preparing for change. Step 4 identifies the specific actions needed to implement the change.

Step 1   In pairs consider the following features of effective schools and effective departments. Use a tick ✓, cross ✗ or unsure ? to identify the strengths and weakness of your department or subject area in relation to these characteristics.

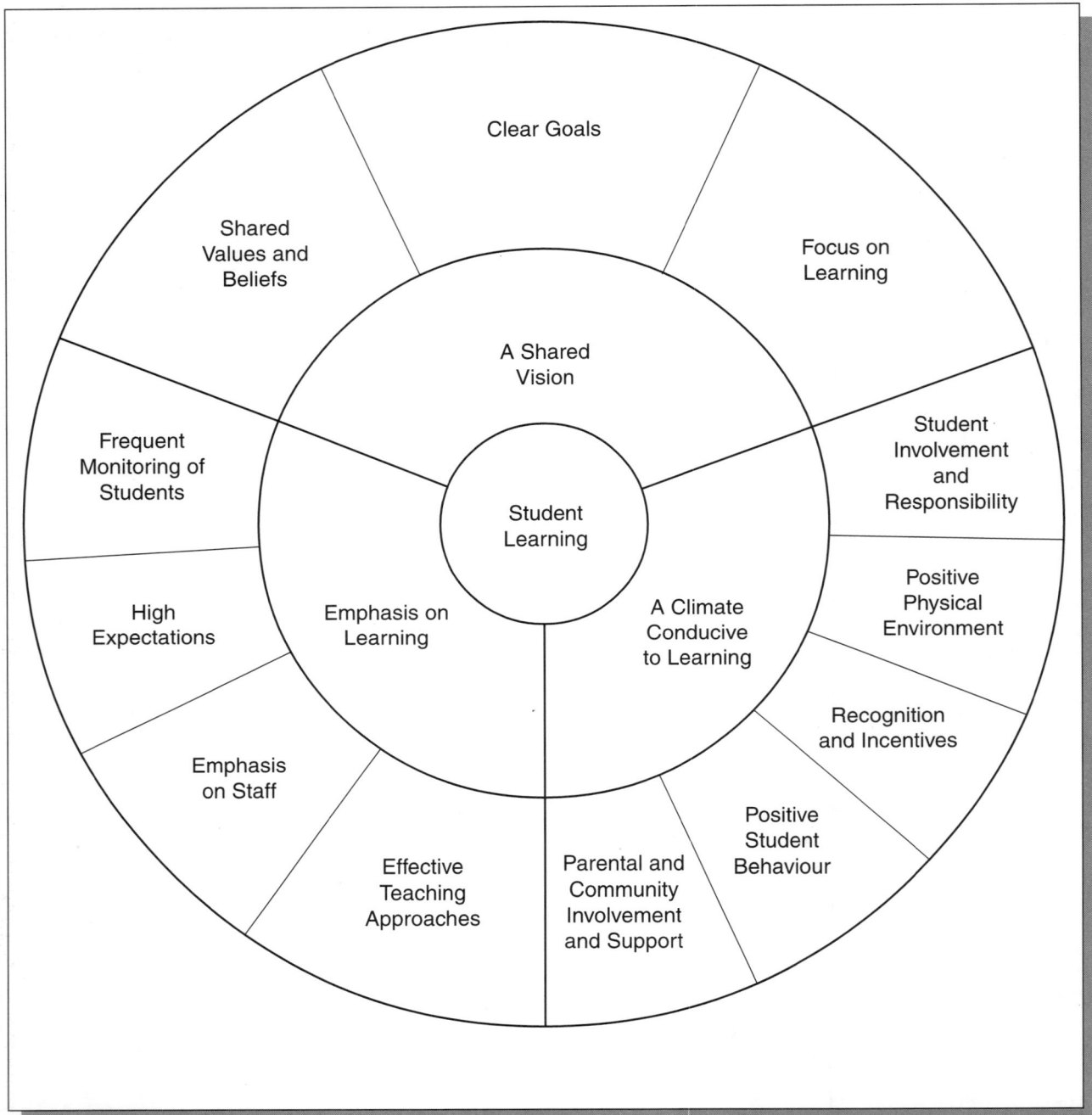

Figure 5.3   Characteristics of effective schools and effective departments
Source: Adapted from Stoll and Fink (1996) and Harris *et al.* (1995)

In pairs compile a list of areas for change and development using the areas marked with a cross as a means of identifying priorities.

Step 2

In pairs, choose one of the priorities for change. Discuss the implications for implementing this change using the checklist of questions below:

Step 3

- How far is the proposed change based upon evidence of a weakness within the department?

- Are you sure you're doing what needs to be done?

- Are teaching and learning at the heart of the proposed change?

- What are the training/staff development implications?

- How will the success of the change be judged?

- How will you tell whether you have made a difference to students?

Step 4 In pairs identify the specific actions now needed to implement the change.

Proposed area of change	Outcomes/evidence
Action 1	
Action 2	
Action 3	
Action 4	

Chapter 6

Improving learning

It is clear from the research that improving the quality of learning should be the main focus of departmental improvement. A major challenge for subject or departmental leaders is to develop and extend the teaching practices used by teachers within their teams in order to meet a range of student learning needs in the classroom. Within any single subject area, teachers are likely to have a range of teaching skills, styles, models and approaches that comprise a teaching repertoire. Different subjects and aspects of subjects necessitate different types of teaching approaches. Consequently, the challenge facing the subject or department leader is how to maximise the effectiveness of teachers within their team and how to ensure that colleagues have the opportunity to extend and develop their individual teaching repertoires. It also means enabling members of the team to select those teaching strategies that are most appropriate for the topic or theme in question.

Currently, teaching approaches tend to be driven by curriculum content. Much teacher time is devoted to 'delivering' the curriculum and relatively little is allocated to considering alternative ways of teaching. However, limited teaching repertoires inevitably mean a narrow set of learning experiences for students. Subject or departmental leaders need to recognise the importance of extending teachers' skills, knowledge and understanding of the learning process (Harris 1999). In order to improve the quality of teaching and learning within the subject area, subject or departmental leaders need, first, to be aware of what constitutes effective learning and how to promote effective learning.

The essence of effective learning lies in the ability of the teacher to edit, merge, revise and re-label what learners already know and to move them forward from this position towards new learning. If what is taught does not engage with the learner's previous understanding, it will be ignored and learning will be ineffective. Consequently, effective teaching must take into account the implicit theories which

Introduction

Effective learning

learners hold. These implicit theories can direct learners' attention and can channel their thoughts. These theories are often very stable and resistant to change. They can derive from first-hand experience, informal social interaction and formal tuition or teaching. It is important, therefore, that these implicit theories are made explicit in order for learning to take place.

At its simplest, effective learning occurs when teachers provide a **positive environment** for learning to take place. This will involve providing access to complex concepts within the subject area. Sometimes the barriers to effective learning may lie in the subject matter itself rather than in general qualities of the teaching or learning activities in which learners are engaged. Extrinsic **motivation** comes from the portrayal of the subject as being important, interesting and rewarding. The subject or departmental leader can play a part in ensuring that the subject matter is presented to students with enthusiasm and encouragement. They also need to take the lead in making their subject area accessible to students and demonstrating how to promote effective learning within the subject area.

The importance of **teacher expectations** about students' aptitude and ability to learn upon subsequent performance has been well documented. Subject or departmental leaders have an important role to play in ensuring that the department has high expectations of all students. Where teachers hold high expectations of students' ability, then students are more likely to achieve at this level. Learning theory stresses the importance of individual differences among learners and underlines the need for learners to believe in themselves as learners (Wood 1988). The stronger students' feelings of self-efficacy, the higher the level of achievement. Consequently, subject or department leaders need to encourage colleagues to **reward**, **praise** and **respect** students as a means to improving students' self-esteem and improving their achievement

To learn effectively, students need to be effective gatherers, organisers and expressers of knowledge (Kyriacou 1986). The main channels for gathering knowledge in school are:

- listening;
- reading;
- asking questions;
- discussing.

Effective learning refers to the ability of learners to respond successfully to the tasks that they are set, as well as the tasks they set themselves, in particular:

- to integrate prior and new knowledge;
- to acquire and use a range of learning skills;
- to solve problems individually and in groups;
- to think carefully about their successes and failures;
- to evaluate conflicting evidence and to think critically;
- to accept that learning involves uncertainty and difficulty.

Source Hopkins *et al.* (2001: 11)

In using such a range of learning strategies the learner's ability to take control over their own learning processes improves. The central characteristic of effective teachers is their ability to create effective learners as well as knowledgeable students. Effective teachers teach their students **how to learn** and thus teaching becomes more productive as students are helped to become more effective learners.

Effective teachers teach students how to **synthesise and refine** information and to own it. Effective learners draw information and ideas from their teachers and use learning opportunities effectively. Thus a major role in teaching is to create effective learners. This same principle applies to schools. Effective schools teach students how to learn and as students progress through those schools they become more effective learners. Consequently, effective teaching should be judged not only by how well it achieves certain cognitive, or affective, outcomes but by how well it has increased students' ability to learn.

One thing that distinguishes successful from unsuccessful learners is the ability to recognise and articulate what it is they do not know, or do not understand. The skill of being articulate about intellectual knowledge provides an important strategy for amplifying that knowledge. It actually helps the student to learn as well as providing them with the ability to express what they do know during exams or during discussions and tests.

Recognising and accommodating **individual differences** among learners is an important component of effective teaching and effective learning. It underlines the need for learners to believe in themselves as learners and to accept that they may have a preferred way of learning. The stronger students' feelings of self-efficacy, the higher the level of achievement. Consequently, teachers need to reward, praise and respect students as a means of improving their self-esteem and improving their achievements.

The **opportunity to learn** is an important variable in explaining variations between schools and teachers. An important part of effective teaching is the extent to which learners feel that they are expected to learn and how opportunities to learn are provided. The importance of individual differences among learners underlines the need for learners to believe in themselves as learners. The research shows that the stronger learners' feelings of self-efficacy, the better the level of achievement. If teachers hold positive views about ability and about their teaching skills, they are more likely to produce academic learning in their classrooms. Essentially, the research demonstrates the importance of teacher expectations upon student learning. Where teachers hold high expectations of students' ability, students are more likely to achieve. The research has also consistently shown the importance of the immediate **environment** on learning and students' motivation to learn. In particular, these research studies have highlighted how the environment of the school, and in particular the classroom, is particularly influential on effective student learning.

To date, a vast number of psychological concepts, principles and processes have been identified as underlying aspects of effective learning. The emphasis given to different psychological concepts, principles and processes differs across the various theories and frameworks employed as a basis for instructional psychology. However, as Kyriacou (1986) has pointed out, there are three main aspects of effective student learning:

- The student must be attending to the learning experience.
- The student must be receptive to the learning experience.
- The learning must be appropriate for the desired learning to take place.

Consequently, teachers need to create the conditions within classrooms where these three aspects of learning are fostered and encouraged. Improving departments promote a deep approach to learning where learning is an active process of relating new meaning to existing meaning and involves the accommodation and assimilation of ideas, skills and thoughts. While no single model of learning is appropriate to encompass all learning goals, there are some key elements to an effective learning experience. The experiential learning model developed by Kolb (1984) involves four stages (see Figure 6.1).

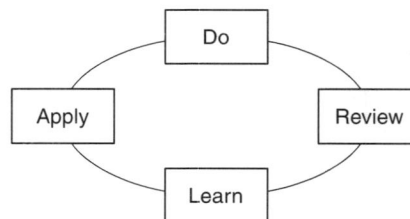

Figure 6.1   Kolb's experiential learning model

This approach to learning emphasises activity in learning (Do), the need for reflection on the learning experience (Review), the making of connections (Learning) and the use of learning in a different context (Apply). Within these four stages the teacher presents a variety of tasks, facilitates and structures reflection, helps learners to make explicit connections and plan the application of learning to new contexts or situations. They also play an important role in gauging student learning through appropriate forms of assessment.

As part of monitoring of learning, subject leaders need to be aware of the assessment practice within the department. In some departments a lack of clear guidance can lead to a situation where in assessment reporting and recording each teacher appears to have an individual system. Departments that are improving pay great care and attention to the assessment process. They have excellent record keeping practices, place a great emphasis on marking consistently within the department, encourage student involvement in the process of marking or assessing where practicable, give feedback to the students and actively seek opportunities to reward good performance (Harris *et al.* 1995).

Many of the assessment practices displayed within improving departments reflect what Stoll and Fink (1996: 124) term 'assessment literacy'. They offer a series of questions for schools and departments to consider:

- Are these the best assessment practices to assess this learning outcome?
- How well does this assessment sample students' achievement?
- Do the students understand the achievement targets and assessment methods?
- Does this assessment assess outcomes that matter?
- Are assessment strategies fair for all students?
- How are the resulting data to be presented?
- Who will have access to the data?
- How will they be reported and to whom?

Assessment must be seen in concert with shifts in curriculum design and teaching strategies. There is little point in designing outstanding learning experiences if the assessment does not capture the learning outcomes required. Stoll and Fink (1996) propose assessment should be based on intended student outcomes with standards of performance determined at the beginning of the teaching–learning process rather than at the end.

Summary

Departments that are improving tend to be those that focus their developmental attention on enhancing teaching and learning. They employ teaching approaches that promote deep learning and encourage students to engage with the process of learning. Improving departments use forms of assessment that require students to reflect upon their own learning and to apply that learning in new or different contexts.

Context

The most effective departments are those which focus increasingly on students' learning. It is clear that departments and subject areas that are improving create the classroom conditions in which effective learning can take place.

Briefing

Aim

To consider how to promote effective learning within the subject area.

Process

This activity is in two parts. Step 1 requires the school, department or group to identify some key elements of learning. Steps 2 and 3 involve planning the subsequent action that needs to be taken to ensure that learning is most effective.

Select a year group you currently teach and identify the key aspects of knowledge, understanding, attitudes and skills needed for this group. Prioritise if necessary.

Step 1

Students in year . . . need to learn the following:

Knowledge

-
-
-
-
-
-
-
-

Understanding

-
-
-
-
-
-
-
-

Attitudes

-
-
-
-
-
-
-
-

Skills

-
-
-
-
-
-
-
-

Step 2   Using this information, discuss what action needs to be taken to ensure that learning is most effective. As a group complete the 'action chart' in Figure 6.2 by outlining how the department or subject area will guarantee effective learning.

Step 3   Use this chart to inform the departmental development plan and as a basis for evaluating departmental progress.

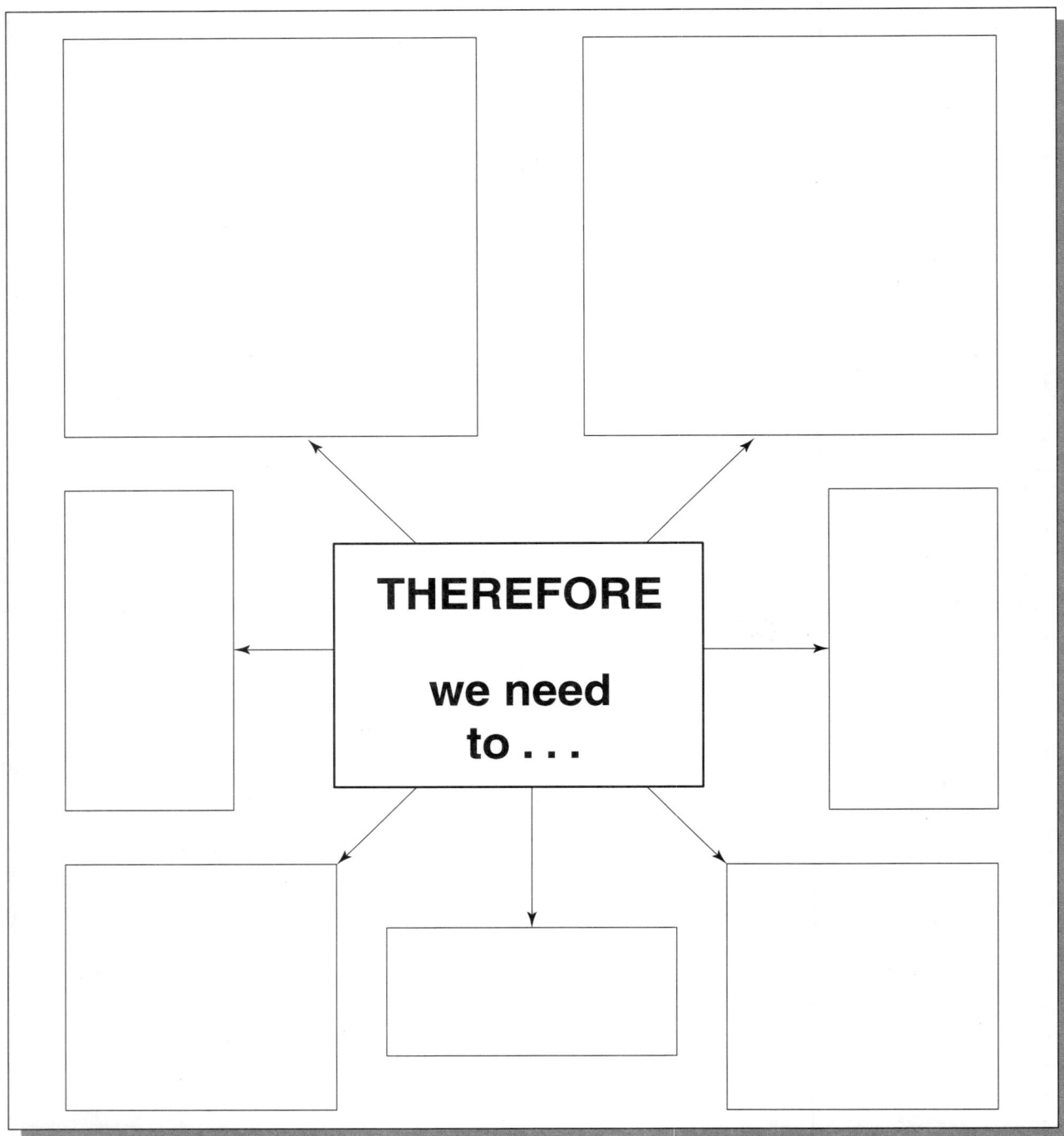

Figure 6.2   Effective learning action chart

Chapter 7

Improving teaching

Research has consistently shown the importance of the classroom environment on learning and students' motivation to learn. It highlights how the teacher influences the learning environment of the classroom and assists students with the process of learning. Within their classrooms, effective teachers create learning environments which foster student progress by deploying their teaching skills as well as a wide range of professional characteristics. As teachers help students acquire information, skills, values and ways of thinking and a means of expressing themselves, they are also teaching them how to learn. It could be argued that the most important long-term outcome of teaching may be the students' increased capacity to learn more easily and effectively in the future. How teaching is conducted has a large impact upon a student's ability 'to learn how to learn'. It has been agreed that effective teachers are not simply charismatic and persuasive presenters but are individuals who engage their students in robust cognitive and social tasks.

The key to being an effective teacher lies in knowing what to do to generate students' learning and achievement. To this end, there have been numerous theories of teaching approaches or styles. However, the effective teacher does not necessarily fit neatly into such categories or typologies. Whatever the relative merits of different teaching approaches or styles, the research findings still reveal little concrete evidence in favour of one approach rather than another. In terms of enhancing teacher effectiveness in the classroom, it would appear that a mixture of approaches or methods is preferable. Indeed, research on teacher effectiveness is still relatively consistent in emphasising the importance of having a range or repertoire of different teaching approaches.

Classroom studies of teaching effects have generally supported a direct and structured approach to teaching. The literature is consistent on the fact that effective teachers:

Introduction

Effective teaching

57

- begin lessons with a review of relevant previous material and a preview of what is to be learned;
- present material in small steps with clear and detailed explanations and active student practice after each step;
- guide students in initial practice by asking questions and checking for understanding;
- provide systematic feedback and correction;
- supervise independent practice;
- provide regular testing and review.

Source: Creemers (1994: 36).

Effective teachers structure the content by beginning with an overview, outlining objectives, calling attention to the main ideas, summarising sub-parts as the lesson progresses and reviewing main ideas at the end. They then guide learners and provide concept maps or summaries to make explicit the connection between the various parts. Effective teachers reinforce learning by repeating and reviewing general rules and concepts. They present clearly, enthusiastically and pace the lesson accordingly.

Effective teachers create an excellent classroom climate and achieve superior student progress largely by displaying more professional characteristics at higher levels of sophistication within a very structured learning environment. From this perspective a teacher promotes learning by being active in planning and organising instruction, explaining to students what they are to learn, arranging occasions for guided practice, monitoring progress, providing feedback, and otherwise helping students to understand and accomplish work. In this role the teacher is the leader and presenter of learning and demonstrates personal attributes, technical competencies and subject knowledge that will promote students' learning in an atmosphere of respect and confidence.

Effective teachers employ a **variety of effective teaching skills** and techniques to engage students and to keep them focused on task. Hay and McBear (2001) note that teaching skills are those 'micro-behaviours' that the effective teacher constantly exhibits when teaching a class. They include behaviour such as:

- using a variety of questioning techniques to probe students' knowledge and understanding;
- involving all the students in the lesson;
- using differentiation appropriately to challenge all the students in the class;
- using a variety of activities or learning methods;
- applying teaching methods appropriate to the National Curriculum objectives.

Teachers are most effective in teaching basic skills when they do the following:

- structure learning experiences;
- proceed in small steps but at a brisk pace;
- give detailed instructions, explanations and examples;

- ask many questions and provide overt student practice;
- provide feedback and corrections, especially in the initial stages of learning new material;
- have a student success rate of 80 per cent or higher, especially in initial learning;
- divide assignments into smaller assignments and find ways to control frequently;
- provide for continued student practice – students may even learn more than is necessary; they may have a success rate of 90–100 per cent and become rapid and self-confident.

The effective teacher communicates the lesson content to be covered and the key activities for the duration of the lesson. Material is presented in small steps, with opportunities for students to practise after each step. Each activity is preceded by clear and detailed instructions. But the planning also takes into account the differing needs of students, including those with specific learning difficulties. For students, there is clarity of what they are doing, where they are going and how they will know when they have achieved the objectives of the lesson. Effective teachers take the time to review lesson objectives and learning outcomes at the end of each lesson. Some describe both the content of the lesson and the learning objectives, and the methods to be employed. But the focus of the planning activity is on student learning outcomes.

Effective teachers are good at setting a clear framework and objectives for each lesson. The effective teacher is very systematic in the preparation for, and execution of, each lesson. The lesson planning is done in the context of the broader curriculum and longer-term plans. It is a very structured approach, beginning with a review of previous lessons, and an overview of the objectives of the lesson linked to previous lessons and, where appropriate, the last homework assignment. Subject and departmental leaders should ask the following questions:

- Does the teacher communicate a clear plan and objectives for the lesson at the start of the lesson?
- Does the teacher have the necessary materials and resources ready for the class?
- Does the teacher link lesson objectives to the National Curriculum?

Effective teachers manage time and resources wisely. The effective management of students, time, resources and support promotes good behaviour and effective learning. Effective teachers achieve the management of the class by having a clear structure for each lesson, making full use of planned time, using a brisk pace and allocating their time fairly among students. Effective teachers start their lessons on time and finish crisply with a succinct review of learning. Effective teachers establish and communicate clear boundaries for student behaviour. They exercise authority clearly and fairly from the outset, and in their styles of presentation and engagement they hold the students' attention. Further questions for the subject and departmental leaders to ask are:

- Does the teacher keep the students on task throughout the lesson?
- Does the teacher correct bad behaviour immediately?
- Does the teacher praise good achievement and effort?
- Does the teacher treat different children fairly?
- Does the teacher structure the lesson to use the time available well?
- Are appropriate learning resources used to enhance students' opportunities?
- Does the teacher use an appropriate pace?

It is evident that effective teachers employ a range of methods and techniques to monitor students' understanding of lessons and work. These could be tests, competitions, questioning or regular marking of written work. Effective teachers look for gains in learning, gaps in knowledge and areas of misunderstanding through their day-to-day work with students. Also, effective teachers encourage students to judge the success of their own work and to set themselves targets for improvement.

Effective teaching involves creating a learning environment which:

- emphasises learning goals and makes them explicit;
- outlines learning purposes and potential learning outcomes;
- carefully organises and sequences curriculum experiences;
- explains and illustrates what students are to learn;
- frequently asks direct and specific questions to monitor students' progress and check their understanding;
- provides students with ample opportunity to practise;
- gives them prompt feedback to ensure success and corrects errors;
- reviews regularly and holds students accountable for work.

Source: Harris (1999)

Another important aspect of effective teaching is ensuring that the students' previous learning is matched to the current learning context. If a teacher is to give maximum opportunity for effective learning, then it is important to consider how to design learning so that all students are able to learn. Teachers have a range of teaching skills, styles, models and approaches that comprise a teaching repertoire. Some teachers have different sets of teaching skills or abilities. Consequently, to maximise the effectiveness of teachers requires presenting opportunities to extend and develop their individual teaching repertoires. This can be achieved by providing opportunities to engage teachers in discussion about teaching methodology and structured reflection about teaching. For optimum professional development to occur, strategies for reviewing and sharing teaching practices are of paramount importance.

Classroom observation

Within any subject or departmental team, teachers' expertise and practical competence will vary. In addition, different subjects use quite different teaching approaches and instructional strategies.

Consequently, classroom observation is an important tool in supporting the professional growth of teachers (Day 1999). It offers a prime source of professional feedback, necessary for improvement and the opportunity to engender and develop a language about teaching simply through talking to others about what happens in classrooms. Classroom observation also combines reflection for the individual teacher and collaborative enquiry for pairs or groups of teachers. It encourages the development of a language for talking about teaching and provides a means for working on developmental priorities for the staff as a whole.

Not only do we learn more about children and their learning by observing, we also learn more about the learning process and our involvement in it.

In setting up a classroom observation process there are a number of questions that the subject or departmental leader needs to consider:

- Who observes?
- What will be observed?
- When will the observation take place?
- How will the observation be recorded?
- What will happen after the observation?
- How will feedback be given?
- How will colleagues respond to the introduction of classroom/ peer observation?

There is an inevitable tension between accountability and development that exists within the observation process. The use of classroom observation within the appraisal process has had the unfortunate consequence of equating observation with notions of accountability. Subject and departmental leaders will need to dispel such interpretations if they are to succeed in using observation in a developmental way. Hence, it is important that any observation process must be transparent from the outset and introduced as a means of professional development, rather than professional evaluation.

What type of observational process will be used? There are different methods of classroom observation: open, focused, and structured. In an open observation, the observer simply notes what appears to them to be important, or relevant. In an observation of this kind, ideas, issues or concerns are noted by the observer in an unstructured way. The limitation of this type of observation is the variability of the evidence base and the diversity of foci noted by the observer.

An alternative to this unstructured approach is a more focused approach where the foci for observation are predetermined and categories exist for recording information. This acts as a filter for the observation process and offers a clearer basis for feedback following the observation. Examples of using observation of this type could be to focus upon questioning techniques, or the interaction of teachers and students. The result of collecting information of this type can be used for discussion with a view to improving teaching.

If the purpose of the observation is to enhance and develop the teaching repertoires of members of the subject team, then the observation must focus upon those teaching skills, approaches and models that are central to the teaching repertoire. It is essential, therefore, that a clear focus for the observation is both identified and agreed with colleagues. Subject leaders will need to encourage colleagues to focus upon some aspect of their teaching that they want to develop further. Hence, observation becomes developmental rather than judgmental and has a real chance of changing teaching behaviour.

Classroom observation need not involve the observation of complete lessons. Many useful insights can be gained from ten or fifteen minutes' worth of observation in a colleague's classroom. The purpose of any observation is to gain insights that will provide the basis for constructive feedback. For example, the observation may focus on:

- the first ten minutes of the lesson, focusing on how the work was initiated and the nature of the students' response;
- the final ten minutes of a lesson, focusing on students' task-related behaviour;
- a particular group of students during group work, focusing on student–student interaction;
- the content of teacher talk versus student talk;
- the nature and content of teacher questions.

Setting up a peer observation system within the subject area requires the subject leader to be clear with colleagues about the reasons for setting up the process. Where observation fails, it is often as a result of a lack of understanding about the purposes behind the process. Subject and departmental leaders need to reassure team members that the reasons for the observation are:

- sharing;
- development;
- support;
- enquiry.

Also, the Head of Department needs to ensure that there are clear ground rules associated with the observation process. A set of questions establishing the ground rules might be as follows:

- Is the focus of the observation clear?
- Are the intentions clear?
- Is there an agreed means of recording?
- Is there an agreed procedure for providing feedback?
- Are confidentiality and trust assured?
- Is there a code of classroom conduct for the observation?

In order to use observation to improve the quality of teaching and learning, it is important that both observer and observed agree the focus of the observation. Within a classroom setting it will be impossible to look at all aspects of teaching and learning, hence a specific focus is necessary. Classroom observation is an important source of information for the evaluation of change and of improvement in classroom practice. It is a highly skilled activity that involves much more than just watching or listening. It involves recording and capturing critical moments in the teaching and learning interactions within classrooms. Observation is central to the teachers' understanding of the classroom and is therefore an essential component of school self-evaluation.

Despite the well-established benefits of peer observation, there will be situations in which the opportunity to engage in observation will not be welcomed. Where observation is used as a mechanism for accountability rather than development, resistance to observation will inevitably ensue.

The main challenge for the subject or department leader is to encourage team members to view observation as an opportunity to learn about their own teaching practices and a means of improving their teaching. If this is achieved, then there is evidence to suggest that improved student learning and increased performance within the department and subject area will ensue.

Summary

Improving the quality of learning should be a goal for all subject and departmental leaders. This is best achieved when teachers have a wide range of teaching strategies from which they can choose wisely according to student and curricular need. These teaching strategies can be developed and enhanced through professional development opportunities such as classroom observation. Subject and departmental leaders have a major role to play in assisting teachers within their team to invest in their own professional learning.

Context

An effective lesson is one where the teacher knows exactly what he or she wants to achieve and can relay this with confidence and enthusiasm to students. It is a lesson that has clearly identified learning outcomes that are shared with students.

Briefing

Aims

To practise classroom observation and to generate criteria for effective teaching within the department/subject area.

Process

This activity involves four steps. Step 1 requires participants to generate a set of criteria for effective teaching within the subject area. Step 2 involves observing a teacher in action using these criteria. Step 3 involves reflection on the observation. Step 4 requires the department to produce an agreed set of criteria for observing colleagues within the department or subject area.

In pairs, generate a list of criteria for effective teaching within your subject area.   *Step 1*

Effective teaching involves:

Effective teaching should be:

Effective teaching results in:

Effective teaching is identified by:

Step 2   Use the criteria to make comments on a video recording of a teacher in action.

During the observation the observer will also need to make notes upon:

- the pace of the lesson;
- the clarity of exposition;
- the classroom activities;
- student engagement;
- classroom management.

In pairs, reflect upon the observation exercise and share views about **_Step 3_** the quality and effectiveness of the teaching. Consider the following:

- whether you have only made negative comments;
- how far your teacher effectiveness criteria could be applied in practice;
- how far your judgement was impartial and fair;
- the limitations of one observation process as a basis for judging teacher effectiveness;
- what constructive feedback you might give the teacher.

Step 4   As a team share the teacher effectiveness criteria generated by the exercise and agree a set of criteria for observation purposes within the department or subject area.

Effective teaching criteria
e.g Teacher provides appropriate learning
   activities for students

Observable features
Students on task for the majority of the
   lesson

Chapter 8

Improving the department

Much is known about the characteristics or features of effective departments but less is known about how departments or subject areas become effective. The way in which individual departments improve might vary but there are some key components of departmental improvement. In terms of improving departments or subject areas, recognising and identifying departmental culture or type is an important first stage. In order to make a department more effective or to improve it, initially it is necessary to **diagnose** the cultural type of the department in question. Research has shown that ineffective departments or subject areas have particular cultures that are at odds with the dominant culture of the school. They tend to be cultures where dissonant values emerge, rendering them fragmented and separate.

Effective departments or subject areas tend to hold a balance between **maintenance** and **developmental** activities. Their maintenance activities are the routine or 'everyday' activities needed to keep the department or subject area operating. The developmental activities are those activities required to ensure the growth of the department. Using these two dimensions it is possible to create a typology of subject or departmental culture, as shown in Table 8.1.

Table 8.1 Typology of departmental culture

	High development	Low development
high maintenance	improving department	stuck department
low maintenance	dynamic department	failing department

Adapted from: Hopkins *et al.* (1994) and Stoll and Fink (1996)

Studies of effective departments or subject areas have shown that they tend to be well organised with efficient systems for recording and reviewing progress. They place a high emphasis on maintenance and are good at the 'day-to-day' routine management tasks and requirements.

In addition, these departments or subject areas are actively involved in their own development but select areas for development and change very carefully. Where there is a balance between maintenance and development to be made, it is most likely that the department or subject area is constantly improving and moving forward.

The failing department

At the other end of the spectrum is the visibly failing department which is low on development and low on maintenance. These departments or subject areas are poor at the day-to-day management tasks and tend to be last minute in their approach to deadlines or problem solving. The lack of leadership in such departments or subject areas means that the necessary organisation and planning is not in place. In addition, the culture of fragmentation evident in these departments or subject areas means that development is not possible as the fundamental infrastructure necessary to support such development is not in place. These failing departments or subject areas are not collegiate and do not have clearly articulated goals, plans and a vision.

The stuck department

Stuck departments are those that undertake all the necessary maintenance activities but neglect developmental work. These departments or subject areas are not obviously failing as they appear to be efficiently run. However, their reluctance to develop or to take on new ideas means that they will, at best, remain where they are and, at worst, gradually deteriorate. Without investment in their development, such departments or subject areas will remain rather pedestrian and will be unlikely to improve. Without any developmental activity these departments or subject areas remain 'sleeping giants' in so far as they have the potential to make an enormous contribution to student performance and achievement but will not unlock that potential without investment in development.

The dynamic department

Dynamic departments or subject areas tend to be those that approach new developments with great enthusiasm and are viewed within the school in a positive way. They tend to be viewed by teachers and students as lively and exciting. These departments or subject areas like to see themselves as 'go ahead' and dynamic but often drive forward innovation at the expense of maintenance activities. On the surface such departments or subject areas might be mistaken as moving because of their high level of involvement in change and innovation. But the opportunity cost of high levels of development is the neglect of basic maintenance activities. Dynamic departments, however, can also be places where fragmentation and disorganisation operate underneath the surface although this is rarely visible. In time these departments will deteriorate because of the lack of emphasis upon maintenance activity and it is likely that the constant drive for innovation and change will lead to feelings of stress, high turnover and possible burnout among team members.

The potential for improvement at the department level to influence improvement at the school level is widely acknowledged. Consequently, there is an imperative to secure improvement across all departments in order to maximise student achievement and learning. Within departmental improvement there are three basic stages:

- diagnosis
- development
- drive

The first stage involves diagnosing the cultural type of the department or subject area. How far is the department demonstrating those features of the improving, stuck, dynamic or failing department? This **diagnosis** or analysis of departmental culture inevitably leads to a consideration of developmental strategies for improvement. The strategies selected will depend upon the individual department's capacity for change. In brief, departments at different stages of **development** will require different improvement strategies not only to enhance their capacity for development, but also to provide a more effective education for their students. Finally, as these developmental strategies are put in place, it will be necessary to employ the necessary **drive** to ensure that the changes are fully implemented.

In selecting the strategies for development and improvement it is important to ensure that they relate directly to the needs of the department and reflect the particular needs of the culture in question. Some suggested strategies for improving different types of department are as follows.

The failing department

Research concerning ineffective departments is not extensive but the work that does exist demonstrates that failing departments need high levels of external support (Harris 1998, 1999). Within these departments a number of early interventions and changes need to be made which have a direct focus upon basic organisational issues. These include:

- changes in leadership;
- engaging external support;
- investing in data and diagnosis;
- securing visible change.

- *Changes in leadership*. It is too sweeping to say that the heads of failing departments do not have the capacity to be effective department leaders. It is, however, certain that they do not have the capacity to resurrect those departments and therefore are potentially a part of the problem. Research suggests that leadership is, to some extent, context-related, so failing departments need changes in leadership practices. Poor management and inappropriate leadership approaches are a consistent feature of ineffective departments (Harris 1998). Consequently, the overall style of leadership needs to be changed in that particular context and new leadership opportunities will need to be created for different staff, using new models, to achieve new goals.

- *Engaging external support*. Departments in a failing situation are likely to be isolated and in a state of cultural stasis. They are unlikely to have the potential for constructive self-analysis or evaluation and will need support from outside to provide knowledge about department improvement strategies and models of ways of working. It is important, however, that the department has some ownership over the selection of the external support and should be able to choose from a range of providers considered to be most suited to its needs.
- *Investing in data and diagnosis*. For improvement strategies to be most effective, the process of data collection and diagnosis is an important first step. Most ineffective departments will need to collect and analyse data to find out why they are unsuccessful and where to direct their efforts for greatest improvement. Data would need to be gathered at whole department level, at departmental level and at classroom level in relation to individual students and groups of students. The purpose of this data collection exercise would be to locate existing good practice within the department to build upon it. This approach has the potential to give the department community ownership of the improvement agenda and to move the problem away from individuals to a whole department focus.
- *Securing visible change*. Following a period of low morale, small, visible changes will demonstrate that things are different in the department. These changes should reflect the core values that the new leadership is articulating. Evidence would suggest that such early indicators of a climate change in the department are important in sustaining further improvement. They have a symbolic and real function, in so far as they show that change is taking place and that a new and different department culture is emerging.

The dynamic department

The dynamic department is possibly the most difficult to improve because it will be seen as a department that is already 'go ahead' and moving. Within this type of department any intervention or change needs to focus upon maintenance and routine organisation. This includes:

- focusing on infrastructure;
- reviewing monitoring and evaluation systems;
- prioritising development;
- seeking external support.

- *Focusing on infrastructure*. Much of the evidence concerning the improvement of dynamic departments points to an emphasis upon managing internal systems rather than responding to external demands (Harris 1998). This means creating the conditions within which maintenance activities can be dealt with most effectively. Strategies for managing maintenance would inevitably include a reallocation of roles and responsibilities throughout the department.

- *Reviewing monitoring and evaluation systems*. Dynamic departments need to review and refine their systems of feedback, namely, monitoring and evaluation. By reviewing monitoring systems the department will be assured that they will receive accurate feedback about the way in which resources are used within the department. Similarly, routine monitoring systems will provide feedback on the extent to which departmental objectives are being met in practice. Evaluation is also a major contributor to departmental and subject planning. Through the evaluation process subject leaders can determine the need to change objectives, priorities and practice. For subject leaders the evaluation of departmental plans can provide the basis for action and strategic intervention.
- *Prioritising development*. Time needs to be set aside for prioritising developmental work and for the sharing of ideas. Consequently, it is important that time is allocated for staff to work together to engage in mutual learning. In this respect, the improvement process needs to be internally supported with expertise and time being given to those within dynamic teams to ensure that the balance and momentum of change are reviewed.
- *Seeking external support*. Isolation from external stimulus and support can be damaging to any department irrespective of its performance level. Dynamic departments need external support to assist them in the process of reviewing systems and developmental priorities. This external support may be offered by the LEA or by the senior management team but it is important that there is the opportunity to review performance and to set new priorities with the help and guidance of someone outside the department.

The stuck department

Research suggests that under-achieving departments need to refine their developmental priorities and focus upon specific teaching and learning issues and build capacity within the department to support this work. These strategies usually involve a certain level of external support, but it is theoretically possible for these departments to improve themselves. Developmental strategies for this type of department include:

- change in leadership approaches;
- improving the environment;
- talking to students;
- sharing values.

- *Change in leadership approaches*. This change incorporates both leadership styles and range. Some restructuring will be necessary in order to diversify leadership opportunities. Department improvement cadres, task groups, multiple team leadership, task-related leadership are strategies which will unlock static structures and systems. Such changes will enable the process of management to become more dynamic and be geared towards increasing the capacity for change.
- *Improving the environment*. Alterations in the department environment can have a dramatic effect on teaching and learning processes. For example, the creation of work areas, enhanced display of students' work, improved social space all indicate to students that the department values them and that they should value the department. The constant reinforcement that learning is valued will contribute to staff morale and can affect student achievement.
- *Talking to students*. Departments are good at internally assessing student effort and achievement. They are less skilled at assessing potential and it is in this gap that the room for improvement lies. The gap between achievement and potential is only meaningful in terms of student life and aspirations. Achievement has to mean something, so formal mechanisms of rewarding all types of student achievement are important and should be built in to any department restructuring programme.
- *Sharing values*. The values and beliefs, of both the profession and the department, need to be articulated and re-affirmed. All staff need to be clear about the value dimension of almost everything that is done in the department. For example, why do we have this assessment system? Why this homework policy? Why these rules or this code of conduct? Why did we deal with this incident in this way? All these decisions will have their roots in the values and beliefs of the department community – and they need to be shared and debated.

The improving department

There has been relatively little debate or research undertaken which has focused upon the improving department. Most attention has been focused on improving poor or low performing departments. However, it is imperative that departments that are improving remain so over time. Consequently, there is a need for specific strategies to ensure the department continues to enhance student performance. These strategies include:

- reinforcing values;
- celebrating success;
- involving students;
- risk-taking.

- *Reinforcing values.* Effective departments should constantly strive to raise expectations (of teachers, students and the wider community) regarding potential student achievement. This means departments need to be explicit, eloquent and prolific in their definition of achievement. They then should celebrate it, communicate it and develop a reward system which will eliminate the need for most sanctions. Such a process will ignite the enthusiasm of staff and generate motivation among students. It is additionally important to give students (and the wider community) ownership of the department's achievements and involve them in organising and participating in regular celebrations of the department's success.
- *Celebrating success.* All departments, at whatever stage in their development, should take joy in every demonstration of success. They should aim to orchestrate optimism and celebration of teacher and student achievement. Everyday professional and social interactions of teachers and students should focus upon the positive rather than the negative, upon success rather than failure, to ensure that this permeates the whole department and every classroom.
- *Involving students.* Once systems, structures, processes, values and professional skills have been developed within the effective department and even when schemes of work and classroom management strategies have been refined, it is still the students who have to take responsibility for their own achievement. It is important that they feel involved and empowered in the process of learning. For example, they can contribute by offering an assessment of teaching and learning processes. By providing their views about how their learning can be improved in the individual classroom and within the department, students are contributing to the improvement process via their constructive feedback.
- *Risk-taking.* Effective departments need to encourage experimentation and risk-taking. They should accept messiness and muddle rather than aim for efficiency. They should subscribe to the view that safe teaching is mundane teaching and aim high and take joy in the successes and talk about the failures. Indeed, real learning lies in understanding the failures rather than the successes.

Summary

The effectiveness of a department can be improved through the selection and implementation of appropriate improvement strategies. It is important that the selected developmental strategies fit the departmental culture and department type. The departmental leader has an important role to play in ensuring that the developmental needs are carefully diagnosed and that appropriate improvement strategies are selected.

Context

Departmental cultures vary and a first step to improvement is the diagnosis of departmental culture.

Briefing

Aim

To identify and evaluate departmental culture.

Process

This activity involves four steps. Step 1 requires an initial diagnosis using the categorisation of improving, stuck, successful and failing. Step 2 considers the action to redress those activities labelled as failing or stuck. Step 3 requires an individual response to the diagnosis of culture, leading to step 4 which involves a discussion of departmental culture and forward planning.

In pairs, using the boxes below identify aspects within your department that fall into the following four categories

Successful	Improving
•	•
•	•
•	•
•	•
•	•
•	•
•	•
•	•
•	•
Stuck	**Failing**
•	•
•	•
•	•
•	•
•	•
•	•
•	•
•	•
•	•

What does this imply about your departmental culture? How might you address those aspects identified within the stuck and failing areas?

Step 3   In pairs, consider the following dimensions of departmental culture and using the questions reflect upon where you would place your department along the positive–negative continuum.

Dimensions of departmental culture			
Positive		**Negative**	**Assessment**
Collaboration	↔	individualism	Do we collaborate to improve and share or do we simply cooperate?
Focus	↔	numerous goals	Do we 'major' on learning and 'minimise' potential distractions?
Learning	↔	behaviour	Do we 'major' on learning or combating misbehaviour?
Can do	↔	fatalism	Do we view change as a series of external impositions or as a series of opportunities by which we can enhance our effectiveness?
Internalisation	↔	externalisation	Are most issues within our department viewed as within our influence/control or are we simply victims of external imposition?
Innovation	↔	resistance to change	Do we accept and build on change to enhance our classrooms?
Supportive culture	↔	blame culture	Do we encourage teachers to try and take risks or are we too ready to blame teachers (and students) who make mistakes?
Feedback	↔	lack of reflection	Do we provide positive and frequent feedback about the details of how we each do our job?
Professional development	↔	individualism	Is professional development including self-critical review a valued element of departmental working?
Quality standards	↔	varied practice	Have we agreed what we stand for and how we will deliver that in day-to-day practice?

Individually complete the review sheet and share with other members of the team as a basis for discussion about departmental culture and a mechanism for planning improvement.

Step 4

Departmental culture – review

Rate your department on the following scale with 1 being the lowest and 10 the highest

Collaboration ↔ individualism

I feel we rate as ....
because we ....
therefore we might help ourselves by ....

Focus ↔ numerous goals

I feel we rate as ....
because we ....
therefore we might help ourselves by ....

Learning ↔ behaviour

I feel we rate as ....
because we ....
therefore we might help ourselves by ....

Can do ↔ fatalism

I feel we rate as ....
because we ....
therefore we might help ourselves by ....

Internalisation ↔ externalisation of the reasons for/the solutions to problems

I feel we rate as ....
because we ....
therefore we might help ourselves by ....

Innovation ↔ resistance to change

I feel we rate as ....
because we ....
therefore we might help ourselves by ....

Supportive culture ↔ blame culture

I feel we rate as ....
because we ....
therefore we might help ourselves by ....

Feedback ↔ lack of reflection

I feel we rate as ....
because we ....
therefore we might help ourselves by ....

Professional development ↔ individualism

I feel we rate as ....
because we ....
therefore we might help ourselves by ....

Quality standards ↔ varied practice

I feel we rate as ....
because we ....
therefore we might help ourselves by ....

Total score ....

Key areas for improvement

-
-
-

Chapter 9

Departmental improvement in action: case studies

Despite growing school improvement literature, there are still relatively few examples of how departments or subject areas improve. While research has shown that there are common features which effective departments or subject areas consistently display (Harris *et al.* 1995; Harris 1999), there is less empirical evidence concerning the process of departmental improvement. Whether departments or subject areas that are improving actively use or reflect on the characteristics of effective departments or subject areas remains questionable. Part of the problem lies in the fact that there are relatively few case studies describing how departments or subject areas improve. While studies that compare departmental performance exist, detailed case studies of the process of improvement are more difficult to find. The following case studies outline how departments improve.

Introduction

Jackie Parker (Deputy Head, Dyffryn Comprehensive School, Newport, Wales)

In my previous school, as a new Head of Department, I was faced with the results for English and English Literature being below national averages. In initial discussions with colleagues, there emerged a consensus that students were not being stretched enough and that the department was not achieving its full potential. It was clear that the Key Stage 4 Curriculum needed revision with an emphasis on a team approach, raising standards and sharing effective teaching practices. The department wanted to build on existing good practice but needed a shared vision which all agreed upon.

The department was facing an inspection and pressure was placed on them to improve. The department agreed that a team ethos and positive vision were essential. If they were to improve, their vision had to be formulated and commonly shared by everyone, therefore it needed to be clear and succinct. On a staff training day five key principles of departmental improvement were agreed:

Case Study One: Improving an English Department

- high expectations of all students;
- a refusal to accept under-achievement;
- all students could enter English and English Literature;
- all students could enter GCSE and achieve real success, many A* – C;
- every individual should be valued.

This became the departmental vision and was used to underpin every aspect of the teaching within the department. It extended to all Key Stages and was shared by every member of the department. Once this vision had been established, the next stage for the department was to develop strategies to make the vision a reality. The strategies employed were as follows:

- *Improving the learning environment*. The department was fortunate to have all English specialist teaching rooms in one block, with plenty of display space. Each teacher had his/her own room and from the beginning great emphasis was placed upon creating a more positive learning environment with students' work attractively displayed to recognise and celebrate both their hard work and high standards. The emphasis was upon displaying the best work of each individual student.
- *Creating a departmental base*. A stock room was transformed into an office/resource area with coffee facilities and working space. This base allowed the department to gather, both formally for meetings and informally to share information, good practice and to develop a team identity. Five years later the resource base has become a computer satellite station as well as a professional office and is constantly used by staff and students.
- *Devolved leadership*. The department agreed to meet weekly for an hour after school in order to create a framework for the department with everyone involved. A collegiate style of management was encouraged with each member of the team taking responsibility for a key departmental area. These included:

  - Key Stage 3 co-ordinator
  - Key Stage 4 co-ordinator
  - Key Stage 5 co-ordinator
  - Special Needs
  - information/communication technology
  - literacy
  - display and competitions
  - resources

  Roles were rotated to foster staff development and to develop new initiatives after consultation. Individual and team strengths were maximised to encourage shared ownership of the department. Trust in each other as colleagues became the cornerstone of creating a positive working environment.

- *Regular departmental meetings*. Weekly meetings were timetabled and focused upon sharing good practice and setting high standards in each of the Key Stages. Meetings, both formal and informal, from the very beginning generated an ongoing dialogue about departmental values. Improvements in communication both within the department and with other departments or subject areas resulted.

- *Raising student expectations.* The department decided that every student would enter English and English Literature, except for a very small minority with particular special needs. They placed an emphasis upon the setting of high, but realistic, targets and acknowledged that success, whether G or an A*, at GCSE is equally valuable because it reflects real achievement for each individual. Almost immediately, the expectations of students, staff and parents were raised across the school. Talking about raising standards took place within the department and a culture of success and expectation was created. As a result, staff and student morale was improved.

- *Monitoring and evaluation.* Regular monitoring and evaluation was undertaken to ensure that each individual was progressing at the right pace and to identify possible under-achievement. The department modified its use of data to allow it to set both possible and probable targets for each individual in each of the Key Stages. This was supported by target setting and mentoring programmes across the school.

- *Target setting.* At Key Stage 3 both short-term and long-term targets were set within the department. National Curriculum levels were targeted each year, looking to build towards GCSE success. Term and annual targets were set with students who were involved in self-assessment and individual target setting. Every opportunity was taken within the department to promote the potential for high achievement. At Key Stage 4 the results of SATs at Key Stage 3 were employed to predict GCSE possible and probable targets. This had been found to 'accelerate' the teaching and the learning processes.

- *Focus on teaching and learning.* The effective organisation of teaching and learning was also fundamental to departmental improvement. Schemes of work and lessons were structured to provide continuity and progression from Year 7 to Year 13. Students were encouraged to mark their own work and to share in the assessment process. Regular feedback to students on every aspect of their work was provided to raise motivation and to encourage even better performance. Students were encouraged to take responsibility for their own learning and progress. Syllabuses and revision guides were shared with them to assist them in developing their own strategies for examination success. Such consistent practices across the department become central to effective departmental working.

The key ingredients of the success of the department are as follows:

- a collegiate management style;
- a clarity of vision;

- clear goals and targets;
- effective teamwork: staff/students/parents/the wider community;
- a climate of success;
- the refusal to accept under-achievement;
- a positive, caring environment;
- valuing students;
- recognising and rewarding achievement;
- monitoring teaching and learning.

Commentary

From this case study, a number of observations can be made. First, that the strategies adopted by the department collectively contributed to a change in departmental culture. It was clear that the department had moved from being a relatively 'stuck' department that accepted students' levels of performance to an improving department that was cohesive and determined that all students should succeed. While such cultural changes take time to achieve, they remain central to sustained school and departmental improvement.

Second, that the leadership style of the Head of Department was critical to successful departmental change. The Head of Department had deliberately adopted a leadership style that was collegiate and required all members of the department to take responsibility for departmental performance. A combination of pressure and support from the Head of Department encouraged staff to strive for continuous improvement.

Finally, there appears to be a high degree of consistency between the actions taken by the department in order to improve and those features identified in the literature as being associated with higher departmental performance. While the characteristics of effective departments or subject areas do not offer any panacea for departmental improvement, this case study would suggest that they have value in framing and guiding strategies for departmental improvement.

Case Study Two: Improving the quality of teaching and learning in the Science Department

Paul Hammond (Deputy Head, Tring School, Tring, Hertfordshire)

This case study outlines the strategies used by effective secondary Heads of Department to positively influence classroom practice. It involved working with the Science Departments of four secondary schools – two in Hertfordshire and two in Bedfordshire. Each of the four departmental leaders nominated three colleagues within the department who had built reputations as effective classroom practitioners. These people were subject to in-depth attention, with each choosing two classes to be interviewed and surveyed for their opinions on what makes an effective science teacher.

In the four departments studied, there was little formal monitoring along the lines of systematic classroom observation or efforts to check on adherence to the departmental policy on the setting of homework. Rather, the departmental leader monitored the quality of teaching and learning through regular informal observation opportunities. Formal procedures would improve classroom provision still further. One department had plans to introduce the monitoring of marking through a sampling of books from across a year group. The anonymous reporting of outcomes at a departmental meeting promised to be a subtle means of departmental leaders nudging teachers towards the expected norm. The culture of trust built up by the departmental leader in question suggested that the introduction of a formal monitoring regime would not disrupt relations with colleagues A combination of both formal and informal approaches would appear to be ideal.

'Vision' is a term often mentioned in connection with effective leadership. The study revealed that those with a clear view of the direction they wanted the department to go had firm ideas on how the vision was best implemented in the context of their department. Interviews with Heads of Department and their colleagues revealed very clear views on the following.

- The nature of Science as a discipline

  I have a commitment to the idea that scientists have a responsibility to let kids know that Science isn't the truth – that Science is speculative – knowledge is therefore always provisional . . . I think that enables kids to see it as a creative activity.

- The manner in which it should be taught

  In as active a way as possible, with students doing as much as possible, practical work wherever they can. In the ideal world as much as can be going on outside of the lesson.

- A wider philosophy of education

  There are values that are inside me – every opportunity I can see I manipulate things so that we get there – students as individual learners and the importance of thinking as opposed to traditional learning of facts and information.

- Views on leadership

  When you stop thinking and challenging what you are doing and why you are doing it – then there's a danger of dying professionally.

- The way that the department should be run

  I think the way he brings the staff together at department meetings – he's not a dictatorial leader – he's very much a person who listens to what the staff have to say but at the same time listens with more of an overall picture of the school – where the school's going.

- And a personal commitment towards living out these values

   He's very enthusiastic – he also leads by example – he's got lots of ideas that he can actually bring across at department meetings – the way he does that – he can get other people involved as well, feeling ownership of it.

Improving teaching and learning

Distinctive actions and attitudes displayed by the Head of Department led to good practice in teaching being identified and adopted consistently across the department. Three common strategies to improve teaching and learning were:

- Developing comprehensive schemes of work

   They form the basis of the lesson we deliver: a list of the learning outcomes; topic broken down into a sensible order; suggestion of resources; experiments; risk assessment and homework.

   The schemes of work – all the materials we produce for these – are the bottom line. The standard below which things should not drop. I am quite happy for people to explore other ways of delivering things as long as they don't fall below this standard.

- Making effective use of department meeting time

   I do think that a departmental or subject leader's job is to think out ways that the department meeting should not get clogged up with administration or discussion of specific points that don't apply to everyone.

   That probably is my most important role in the meeting – to keep a focus on the issues and in advance of the meeting it is to be selective – to filter and decide what are the key things we need to deal with at this time.

- Shaping the culture of the teachers' workroom

   The great strength of it is that people are constantly in a dialogue about the work they are doing – they are taking the tips and advice and basic strategies that make for successful teaching.

The workroom can influence the attitudes of teachers towards students as much as it can inform them about the best resources to use for different activities.

In the room we do talk about students and we hear how people react to certain situations or certain students and there is a sense of caring here – you're not always down on them – that obviously affects you and your relationship with the students. This feeling is established in the department and you are part of that.

Impact on classroom practice

Departmental leaders exert a positive influence on classroom practice where they:

- *resolve* the actual and potential tensions that arise, first of all, within the departmental or subject leader's roles and, second, between their own roles and those of other school personnel;
- *generate* opportunities for good classroom practice to be identified in classroom observation, shared in department meetings and recorded in schemes of work;
- *appreciate* the current capacity of their department for change and development and adopt a suitable management style;
- *develop* trust and respect from colleagues, thus providing the social dynamic necessary for the introduction and maintenance of quality assurance measures.

Commentary

In the schools in the study it was clear that Heads of Departments had a broad vision that encompassed the essence of Science as a discipline; the manner in which it should be taught; a view of departmental management and a commitment to improving classroom practice. In addition, departmental leaders established the department meeting as a channel for professional development with emphasis on the sharing of good practice in teaching and learning.

In these departments schemes of work were used to organise teaching effectively and to document examples of good practice. Departmental leaders encouraged the use of teachers' departmental workrooms as an informal forum for the interchange of professional opinions and information. They also streamlined administrative tasks and encouraged forward planning through measures such as the provision of departmental bulletins and interim discussions with key personnel between the regular departmental meetings. In summary, departmental leaders understood the capacity of their department to change and develop and were willing to pursue appropriate strategies to maximise improvements in teaching and learning.

Chapter 10

The current context

Effective leadership is acknowledged to be of central importance in the pursuit of improved educational standards. The quality of leadership has been shown to be a critical component in securing high levels of school performance. The role of the subject or departmental leader now includes a diverse and pressing set of demands. They are expected to apply professional knowledge, understanding and skills to all the key areas identified within the standards. The importance of the role and the implications for increased work-load are substantial. In addition, there are some inherent tensions within this leadership role

Leader or teacher?

The new responsibilities placed upon subject leaders are extensive and exhaustive. In the majority of schools these responsibilities will prove difficult to fulfil because subject and departmental leaders, unlike other school leaders, have a significant teaching responsibility that competes for time and energy. As a consequence, there will be an inevitable conflict of roles as subject and departmental leaders try to balance teaching with leading their subject area. At worst, subject and departmental leaders will attempt to 'juggle' existing time to meet the requirements of the role or will simply decide that the demands placed upon them are too great and will fail to meet the required standards. If subject and departmental leaders are to be able to work most effectively on behalf of their team members and the school, then additional time would seem to be an important prerequisite.

Leader or manager?

While leadership and management are often seen as inseparable concepts, the functions associated with each are clearly different. Subject and departmental leaders have an operational responsibility for ensuring subject area objectives and targets are met and tasks are

Introduction

completed. These maintenance responsibilities are necessary to run an efficient department or subject area and represent the day-to-day management requirements of the role. In addition, subject and departmental leaders are required to provide a vision for the subject area, to provide clear direction, to motivate others and to inspire and gain the commitment of those within their team. Such leadership qualities are necessary to develop the subject area, to improve achievement and to raise standards. The tension between management and leadership is partly an issue of time and partly an issue of competing priorities. Effective subject and departmental leaders and, indeed, effective school leaders are able to balance management and leadership responsibilities and view them as different rather than competing dimensions of the role.

Leader or follower?

While subject leaders working with their teams are very much in the front line, this does not necessarily mean that they are automatically involved in strategic matters, or school-level decision-making. Levels of involvement vary according to the management approach of senior staff and the way in which both groups interact. The relationship between the middle management layer and the senior management team is critically important in fostering whole school change, yet in the majority of cases there is no formal interface between both groups and communication still tends to be 'top down'. In order to contribute to whole school development, subject and departmental leaders need to be participants in policy development and strategic planning. This requires, first, structural change where a formal 'two-way' equal relationship is established between middle and senior management and, second, cultural change where subject leaders are integrally involved in decision-making and policy developments within the school.

Leader or assessor?

At the core of the subject and departmental leaders' role is improving the quality of teaching and learning. This inevitably involves monitoring subject performance and evaluating the quality of teaching within the subject area. It also necessitates judging teaching performance and, if necessary, challenging 'poor' teaching and unacceptable classroom practices. With performance management, subject and departmental leaders have a more prominent role to play in evaluating teaching and will be increasingly called upon as a source of evidence about teaching capability and competence. However, they also have a major role to play in supporting colleagues within their subject area. Consequently, the challenge facing subject leaders is how to balance accountability and development within the subject area and how to foster a climate of trust among colleagues that allows this balance to be supported and maintained.

Research has shown that the Head of Department can greatly influence the culture of teaching within their subject, or curriculum area (Harris, 1998; Harris, 1999). Whether departments or subject areas work collaboratively or not will largely be dictated by the Head of Department or subject leader. Similarly, the extent to which teachers share common goals and subscribe to a shared vision will be partly dependent upon the Head of Department's management style.

The overall purpose of the subject leader's role is to contribute to school improvement and increased standards of performance through the provision of high quality teaching within the subject area. In order to achieve this, the subject leader has to lead and manage the curriculum and to respond to the internal and external demands for accountability and quality. All these demands have to be met in the particular context of the individual school and the community it serves. Schools operate in very divergent socio-economic, cultural and political settings. Resources, expertise, staff profiles and areas differ quite extensively. Consequently, the major challenge facing all schools is how to ensure that every Head of Department and subject leader has the time, opportunity and support to undertake their complex but essential role.

Final Comment

References and further reading

Busher, H. and Harris, A. (1999) 'Leadership of school subject areas: tensions and dimensions of managing in the middle'. *School Leadership and Management*, 19(3), 305–17.

Busher, H. and Harris, A. (2000) *Leading Subject Areas, Improving Schools*. London: Paul Chapman.

Busher, H. and Harris, A. (2001) 'Leadership of school subject areas: tensions and dilemmas of managing in the middle', in Moon, B., Bird, L. and Butcher, J. (eds) *Leading Professional Development in Education*. London: Routledge.

Creemers, B. P. M. (1994) *The Effective Classroom*. London: Cassell.

Day, C. (1999) *Developing Teachers: the Challenges of Lifelong Learning*. London: Falmer.

Day, C., Hall, C. and Whitaker, P. (1998) *Developing Leadership in Primary Schools*. London: Paul Chapman.

Day, C., Harris, A., Hadfield M., Tolley, H. and Beresford, J. (2000) *Leading Schools in Times of Change*. Milton Keynes: Open University Press.

English, T. and Harris, A. (1987) *An Evaluation Toolbox for Schools*. London: Longman.

Fullan, M. (1991) *The New Meaning of Educational Change*. London: Cassell.

Handy, C. (1976) *Gods of Management*. London: Pan.

Harris, A. (1998) 'Improving the effective department: strategies for growth and development'. *Education Management and Administration*, 26(3), 269–78.

Harris, A. (1999) *Effective Subject Leadership: A Handbook of Staff Development Activities*. London: David Fulton Publishers.

Harris, A. (2000) *Effective Leadership and Departmental Improvement*. Westminster Studies in Education, vol. 23, pp. 81–90.

Harris, A. (2001) 'Department improvement and school improvement: a missing link?' *British Educational Research Journal*, 27(4), 477–87.

Harris, A. Jamieson, I. M. and Russ, J. (1995) 'A study of effective departments in secondary schools'. *School Organisation*, 15(3), 183–229.

Harris, A. Jamieson, I. M. and Russ, J. (1996) *School Improvement and School Effectiveness: A Practical Guide*. London: Pitman.

Harris, A., Jamieson, I. M. and Russ, J. (1997) 'Effective departments or subject areas in secondary schools', in Harris, A., Bennett, N. and Preedy, M. (eds) *Organisational Effectiveness and Improvement*. Milton Keynes: Open University Press.

Hay/McBer (2001) *Effective Teaching*. London: HMSO.

Hopkins, D., Ainscow, M. and West, M. (1994). *School Improvement in an Era of Change*. London: Cassell.

Hopkins, D. and Harris, A. (2001) *Creating the Conditions for Teaching and Learning: A Handbook of Staff Development Activities*. London: David Fulton Publishers.

Hopkins, D., Harris, A., Singleton, C. and Watts, R. (2001) *Creating the Conditions for Teaching and Learning: A Handbook of Staff Development Activities*. London: David Fulton.

Joyce, B. and Weil, M. (1988) *Models of Teaching* (4th edn). Englewood Cliffs, NJ: Prentice-Hall.

Kolb, D. (1984) *Experiential Learning*. London: Prentice-Hall.

Kyriacou, C. (1986) *Effective Teaching in Schools*. Oxford: Basil Blackwell.

Sammons, P., Thomas, S. and Mortimore, P. (1997) *Forging Links: Effective Schools and Effective Departments or Subject Areas*. London: Paul Chapman.

Siskin, L. (1994) *Realms of Knowledge: Academic Departments in Secondary Schools*. London: Falmer.

Stoll, L. and Fink, D. (1996) *Changing our Schools: Linking School Effectiveness and School Improvement*. Buckingham: Open University Press.

Teacher Training Agency (1998) *Standards for Subject Leaders*. London: Teacher Training Agency.

West, M., Jackson, D., Harris, A. and Hopkins, D. (2000). 'Leadership for school improvement', in Riley, K. and Seashore, L. K. *Leadership for Change*. London: Routledge.

Wood, D. (1988) *How Children Think and Learn*. London: Blackwell.

Further Reading

Bennett, N. (1995) *Managing Professional Teachers: Middle Management in Primary and Secondary Schools*. London: Paul Chapman.

Blandford, S. (1997) *Middle Management in Schools*. London: Pitman Publishing.

Gold, A. (1998) *Head of Department Principles and Practice*. Wiltshire: Cassell.

Jones, P. and Sparks, N. (1996) *Effective Heads of Department*. London: Educational Press.

Leask, M. and Tererell, I. (1997) *Development Planning and School Improvement for Middle Managers*. London: Kogan Page.

OFSTED (1997) *Subject Management in Secondary Schools*. London: OFSTED.

Sammons, P., Thomas, S. and Mortimore, P. (1997) *Forging Links: Effective Schools and Effective Departments or Subject Areas*. London: Paul Chapman.

West, N. (1997) *Middle Management in the Primary School*. London: David Fulton Publishers.

Index

leadership (*cont.*)
  change in approaches 74
  changes in 71–2
  changing role 2–4
  devolved 82
  dimensions of role 18–19
  effective 19–20, 23–6
  importance of 1–2
  styles 26, 84
  tensions within role 89–90
  ways to improve 20–2
'leading professional' approach 17
learning 9, 10, 49–56, 83, 86
learning environment 50, 51–2, 57, 60,
    74, 82
learning from others 21
lesson planning 59
liaison or representative role 18

maintenance activities 69, 70, 72–3
management 3, 89–90
meetings 29, 82–3, 86
mentoring or supervisory leadership
    role 18
middle management/senior
    management relationship 90
monitoring
  reviewing systems of 73
  of student progress 8, 9–10, 83
  of teaching 3–4, 90
motivation
  of students 50
  of team 30

National College for School Leadership
    1, 4
National Standards for Subject Leaders
    1, 2, 3

observation 60–3, 64–8
opportunity to learn 51

Parker, Jackie 81–4
personal development planning 21
planning
  change 38
  lessons 59
  personal development 21
potential, student 74
professional development 43
profiles 8
progress, monitoring and evaluating
    student 8, 9–10, 83

relationship roles 30
relationships 18–19, 22
representative or liaison role 18
resistance 37–8
resources, management of 8

risk taking 75
roles 30–1
  conflict of 31
routines and practices, clear 10

schemes of work 8, 9, 86
Science department, case study of 84–7
self-evaluation 8
senior management/middle
    management relationship 90
Stoll, L. 53
strategies for improvement 71–5, 82,
    86
stress, managing 21–2
stuck department 70, 73–4
student-centred ethos 10
Subject Leader Standards 1, 2, 3
success, celebrating 75
supervisory or mentoring leadership
    role 18
support
  external 72, 73
  for colleagues 43–4
supporting leadership style 26
sustaining change 41–2
SWOT analysis 38

'talking departments' 8
talking to students 74
target setting 83
task roles 30
teacher expectations 50, 51
teaching
  approaches 49, 57
  and case studies of departmental
      improvement 83, 86
  classroom observation of 60–3, 64–8
  effective 57–60, 64–8
  in effective departments 9, 10
  monitoring and evaluating 3–4, 90
  skills 58–9
  and subject leader's role 89
teams
  effective 27–8, 33–5
  high performance 28
  phases of team development 28–9
  roles 30–2
  ways to improve 28–30
threats to change 38
transactional leadership role 18
transformational leaders 18

values 19, 74, 75
visible change, securing 72
vision 7–8, 9, 17, 19–20, 81–2, 85
vision statement 20

workroom culture 86
workshop/workplace links 43